ARTIFICIAL INTELLIGENCE WITH PYTHON

Building Intelligent Applications

THOMPSON CARTER

TABLE OF CONTENTS

INTRODUCTION

Artificial Intelligence with Python: Building Intelligent Applications

In the rapidly advancing world of technology, artificial intelligence (AI) stands at the forefront of innovation, reshaping industries, economies, and everyday life. From self-driving cars to personalized recommendation systems, from natural language processing to cutting-edge medical diagnostics, AI is not just a buzzword—it's a transformative force that is rapidly redefining how we interact with the world and each other.

However, for many, AI can feel like a mysterious and complex field—dominated by advanced mathematics, obscure algorithms, and overwhelming jargon. For developers, data scientists, and business professionals eager to leverage the power of AI without getting lost in the technical weeds, the challenge often lies in translating AI concepts into practical, real-world applications. This is where Python comes in. As one of the most accessible and powerful programming languages for AI, Python offers a rich ecosystem of libraries, frameworks, and tools that allow practitioners to seamlessly build, deploy, and scale intelligent applications.

This book, **"Artificial Intelligence with Python: Building Intelligent Applications,"** is designed to provide a comprehensive, jargon-free guide to using Python for AI development. Whether you're an experienced developer looking to expand your skill set, a data enthusiast eager to dive into machine learning, or a business professional curious about AI's practical implications, this book aims to bridge the gap between theory and practice. Through clear explanations, step-by-step guidance, and real-world case studies, this book will walk you through the essential concepts, tools, and techniques you need to build intelligent applications with Python.

Why This Book?

In recent years, AI has become more accessible than ever before. Machine learning models that once required deep expertise and high-performance computing are now being made available to anyone with a laptop and an internet connection. With Python's wide adoption in the AI community, it has emerged as the language of choice for building AI models. Its simplicity and readability, combined with powerful libraries like TensorFlow, Keras, Scikit-learn, and PyTorch, have made it the go-to tool for anyone seeking to harness the power of AI in their applications.

But while there is no shortage of resources on AI and Python, many existing tutorials and books dive deep into technical theory, leaving out the practical steps required to build and deploy real-world applications. Moreover, they often assume a high level of familiarity with mathematics and statistical concepts, which can alienate beginners and even intermediate developers who are more focused on applications than on abstract theory.

This book takes a different approach. While we will cover the foundational concepts of AI, we will focus on practical, real-world applications that can be immediately put into practice. We will explore how Python can be used to build a wide range of intelligent systems—whether it's a machine learning model that predicts customer behavior, a deep learning model for image recognition, or a chatbot that powers customer service. Each chapter is designed to build upon the last, guiding you through the entire process of developing AI systems, from initial setup and data handling to model building and deployment.

Who Is This Book For?

This book is aimed at a broad audience—from beginners to experienced practitioners—who are interested in learning how to use Python to build AI-powered applications. Here's a closer look at who will benefit from this book:

- **Developers and Data Scientists**: If you're a developer with some experience in Python but are new to AI or machine learning, this book will give you the tools and frameworks you need to get started. You'll learn how to use popular Python libraries and frameworks to build and deploy intelligent applications. For data scientists who are familiar with basic machine learning but want to dive deeper into advanced AI techniques (like neural networks and reinforcement learning), this book offers practical case studies to build your expertise.

- **Business Professionals and Entrepreneurs**: If you're a business professional or entrepreneur interested in applying AI to solve real-world problems (whether it's customer segmentation, fraud detection, or predictive analytics), this book will help you understand the underlying concepts of AI without overwhelming you with technical jargon. You'll learn how to identify opportunities for AI in your industry, and how to communicate effectively with technical teams to implement AI solutions.

- **Students and Educators**: If you're a student or educator exploring AI, this book will provide you with a practical, hands-on approach to learning. The step-by-step examples and real-world case studies will help solidify your understanding of key AI concepts, making them more tangible and applicable to real-life projects.

What Will You Learn?

Over the course of the 24 chapters, this book will guide you through the essential components of building AI systems with Python:

1. **Understanding AI Fundamentals**: We'll start by introducing the core concepts of AI, machine learning, and deep learning, helping you develop a solid understanding of these fields. We'll also explore why Python is such a powerful tool for AI development and introduce you to the key libraries that make Python the language of choice for AI.

2. **Working with Data**: Data is the backbone of AI. You'll learn how to collect, clean, and analyze data to ensure it's ready for machine learning models. We'll explore techniques for data preprocessing, feature engineering, and visualization using libraries like Pandas, Matplotlib, and Seaborn.

3. **Building Machine Learning Models**: You'll dive into the world of machine learning, learning how to build and train models for tasks like classification, regression, and clustering. You'll see how to use popular Python libraries such as Scikit-learn to build your first machine learning models and evaluate their performance.

4. **Deep Learning and Neural Networks**: We'll explore how to build deep learning models using libraries like Keras and TensorFlow. You'll learn about neural networks, convolutional neural networks (CNNs) for image recognition, and recurrent neural networks (RNNs) for time-series data and natural language processing.

5. **Advanced AI Techniques**: For those looking to take their skills further, we'll explore advanced techniques like reinforcement learning, transfer learning, and generative models. You'll see how these techniques are applied in real-world scenarios such as game development, robotics, and creative AI.

6. **Deploying AI Models**: One of the most critical aspects of AI development is getting your models into production. We'll cover best practices for deploying machine learning models at scale, using cloud services like AWS, Google Cloud, and Azure. You'll also learn how to integrate AI models into web and mobile applications using frameworks like Flask and Django.

7. **Ethics and Future of AI**: Finally, we'll take a step back to explore the ethical implications of AI. As AI becomes more ubiquitous, it's crucial to understand its potential impact on privacy, fairness, and accountability. We'll also look ahead to the future of AI, examining emerging trends such as Artificial General Intelligence (AGI), quantum computing, and the role of AI in solving global challenges.

Why Python for AI?

Python's rise to prominence in the AI field can be attributed to its simplicity, readability, and the availability of a robust ecosystem of libraries and frameworks. Libraries like **Scikit-learn**, **TensorFlow**,

Keras, and **PyTorch** provide powerful, easy-to-use tools that abstract away the complexities of building machine learning and deep learning models, allowing developers to focus on problem-solving and innovation. Furthermore, Python's strong support for data manipulation (via **Pandas**), visualization (via **Matplotlib**, **Seaborn**), and scientific computing (via **NumPy** and **SciPy**) makes it a versatile choice for AI development.

The world of AI is vast, exciting, and full of potential. Whether you are looking to build intelligent applications that improve business processes, solve complex real-world problems, or simply understand the workings behind cutting-edge AI technologies, this book provides the tools, techniques, and knowledge to help you succeed. By focusing on Python—one of the most accessible and powerful tools for AI development—and emphasizing practical, real-world examples, we hope to equip you with everything you need to bring your AI ideas to life.

Let's embark on this journey into the world of artificial intelligence, and explore the limitless possibilities it offers for innovation and discovery.

CHAPTER 1: INTRODUCTION TO AI AND PYTHON

This first chapter sets the stage for the book by introducing the fundamental concepts of Artificial Intelligence (AI) and explaining why Python has become the go-to language for AI development. It will also cover key libraries and tools that will be used throughout the book to build intelligent applications.

1.1 Overview of AI Concepts

What is AI? Artificial Intelligence refers to the simulation of human intelligence processes by machines, particularly computers. AI is broadly divided into two categories:

- **Narrow AI (Weak AI):** Systems designed to handle a specific task or a narrow range of tasks. Examples include speech recognition systems (e.g., Siri), image classification, and self-driving cars.
- **General AI (Strong AI):** A theoretical form of AI that could perform any intellectual task that a human being can. While this remains largely speculative and is the subject of ongoing research, it represents the ultimate goal of AI.

Core Areas of AI: AI spans a variety of subfields, each addressing different aspects of human cognition. Key areas include:

- **Machine Learning (ML):** A method of data analysis that automates analytical model building. Machine learning algorithms enable computers to improve from experience without being explicitly programmed.
- **Deep Learning (DL):** A subset of machine learning based on artificial neural networks. Deep learning has become especially popular in tasks such as image and speech recognition.
- **Natural Language Processing (NLP):** A field of AI focused on enabling machines to understand, interpret, and respond to human language. Applications include chatbots, sentiment analysis, and language translation.
- **Computer Vision (CV):** The field that enables machines to interpret and make decisions based on visual input. It includes tasks such as object detection, image segmentation, and facial recognition.
- **Reinforcement Learning (RL):** A type of learning where agents learn by interacting with their environment and receiving rewards or penalties. It's commonly used in robotics and autonomous vehicles.

1.2 Why Python is Ideal for AI Development

Simplicity and Readability: Python's syntax is clear, straightforward, and easy to learn, making it an ideal choice for both beginners and experienced developers. This simplicity allows developers to focus on building algorithms rather than dealing with complex programming constructs.

Extensive Ecosystem of Libraries and Frameworks: Python has a rich ecosystem of libraries and frameworks that simplify AI development. Libraries like NumPy, Pandas, and Matplotlib make it easy to handle data, while specialized AI libraries like TensorFlow, PyTorch, and Scikit-learn provide powerful tools for building and deploying machine learning and deep learning models.

Community and Support: Python has one of the largest and most active programming communities in the world. This means developers can easily find tutorials, documentation, forums, and open-source projects that accelerate the development of AI applications.

Cross-platform Compatibility: Python works seamlessly across different platforms, from Windows to Linux and macOS, making it a versatile choice for AI developers who may need to deploy applications on various systems.

Integration with Other Languages: Python integrates easily with other programming languages like C++ and Java, which is useful when performance-critical components need to be implemented in lower-level languages.

1.3 Key Libraries and Tools for AI Development

Throughout the book, we'll work with several libraries and tools that are essential for building AI applications. Here's a brief overview of the key libraries you'll encounter:

1.3.1 TensorFlow

- **Overview:** Developed by Google, TensorFlow is one of the most popular deep learning frameworks. It provides an extensive set of tools for building and training machine learning models, including support for both low-level operations and high-level APIs like Keras.
- **Why it's useful:** TensorFlow is highly scalable and supports both CPU and GPU computations. It's used for tasks like image recognition, natural language processing, and even reinforcement learning.

1.3.2 PyTorch

- **Overview:** PyTorch is another deep learning framework that is widely used in research and production environments. It's known for its dynamic computation graph, which allows for more flexibility in model development.

- **Why it's useful:** PyTorch is user-friendly and allows for seamless debugging, making it a popular choice for research and prototyping. It's particularly favored in academia due to its ease of use and flexibility.

1.3.3 Scikit-learn

- **Overview:** Scikit-learn is a powerful, easy-to-use library for machine learning in Python. It includes a wide variety of algorithms for classification, regression, clustering, and dimensionality reduction.
- **Why it's useful:** Scikit-learn is great for beginners because of its simple interface, yet powerful enough for advanced applications. It supports a range of machine learning models, including decision trees, support vector machines, and k-means clustering.

1.3.4 Pandas

- **Overview:** Pandas is a library used for data manipulation and analysis. It provides data structures like DataFrame that allow for easy handling of structured data.
- **Why it's useful:** Pandas simplifies tasks like data cleaning, exploration, and transformation. It's an essential tool for preparing data before feeding it into AI models.

1.3.5 NumPy

- **Overview:** NumPy is a library for numerical computing in Python. It provides support for large, multi-dimensional arrays and matrices, along with a variety of mathematical functions to operate on these arrays.
- **Why it's useful:** NumPy is the backbone for numerical computations in Python and is used extensively in machine learning and AI for data manipulation, matrix operations, and linear algebra.

1.3.6 Matplotlib and Seaborn

- **Overview:** Matplotlib is a plotting library used to create static, animated, and interactive visualizations in Python. Seaborn, built on top of Matplotlib, provides a higher-level interface for drawing attractive statistical graphics.
- **Why they're useful:** These libraries are essential for data visualization, allowing you to explore and communicate patterns in the data. Visualizations can be crucial in interpreting AI model results and data distributions.

1.3.7 Jupyter Notebooks

- **Overview:** Jupyter Notebooks provide an interactive environment for writing and executing Python code. They allow you to document your code, run experiments, and visualize results in a notebook-style format.

- **Why it's useful:** Jupyter is popular among data scientists and AI practitioners for prototyping and experimenting with models. It's especially useful for AI projects, where you might need to tweak and visualize results iteratively.

1.4 Getting Started with AI Development in Python

Now that we've covered the basics of AI and the Python ecosystem, it's time to set up the development environment. In the next chapter, we'll dive into installing Python, setting up your IDE, and getting started with the first few lines of code. But first, it's important to understand that AI development is an iterative process. You'll often start with a basic model and refine it based on results, which makes Python's flexibility and support for rapid prototyping so valuable.

- AI is about creating machines that can simulate human intelligence, and it is divided into subfields such as machine learning, deep learning, NLP, and computer vision.
- Python is the ideal language for AI because of its simplicity, extensive libraries, and strong community support.
- Key libraries like TensorFlow, PyTorch, Scikit-learn, Pandas, and Matplotlib provide the essential tools for building AI applications.

In this chapter, we've laid the groundwork for your AI journey, and in the following chapters, we will start building more complex AI systems using Python.

This chapter should provide a strong foundation for the rest of the book, ensuring readers understand the key concepts and tools before diving into practical examples and deeper learning in subsequent chapters. Let me know if you'd like to refine any section!

CHAPTER 2: THE BUILDING BLOCKS OF AI

In this chapter, we will dive into some of the fundamental concepts of machine learning and deep learning, which are the backbone of AI. We'll explore the different types of machine learning, including supervised and unsupervised learning, and introduce the basics of deep learning and neural networks.

2.1 Basic Machine Learning Concepts

What is Machine Learning? Machine learning (ML) is a branch of AI that focuses on building systems that learn from data rather than being explicitly programmed to perform specific tasks. At its core, ML involves creating algorithms that can identify patterns in data and make predictions or decisions based on that data.

The process generally involves three steps:

1. **Data Collection:** Gathering the data needed to train the model.

2. **Model Training:** Using the data to teach the algorithm by finding patterns.

3. **Prediction/Inference:** Using the trained model to make predictions or decisions on new, unseen data.

Types of Machine Learning: Machine learning can be broadly classified into three main types based on the learning style and available data:

1. **Supervised Learning:** The model is trained on labeled data, meaning the input data is paired with the correct output (labels). The goal is to learn the relationship between input and output to predict the output for new data.

   o **Example:** Predicting house prices based on features like location, size, and number of bedrooms. The dataset includes the actual prices of the houses (labels).

2. **Unsupervised Learning:** The model is trained on unlabeled data, meaning the algorithm must discover patterns and

structures in the data on its own. It tries to group or cluster the data based on similarities.

- **Example:** Customer segmentation in marketing, where the algorithm groups customers based on purchasing behavior without knowing any predefined labels.

3. **Reinforcement Learning:** The model learns by interacting with its environment and receiving feedback in the form of rewards or penalties. It is often used in game-playing AI or robotics.

- **Example:** An AI agent learning to play chess by making moves, receiving rewards (win), or penalties (loss) based on its actions.

2.2 Supervised vs Unsupervised Learning

Supervised Learning

In supervised learning, the training dataset consists of input-output pairs. The input (features) is accompanied by the correct output (label), and the model learns to predict the output based on the input.

- **Use Cases of Supervised Learning:**
  - **Classification:** Categorizing data into predefined classes. For example, spam email detection (spam or not spam) or medical diagnosis (diseased or healthy).
  - **Regression:** Predicting continuous values. For example, predicting the stock price or house price based on historical data.

Common Algorithms:

- **Linear Regression:** Used for regression tasks where the relationship between the input variables and the output is assumed to be linear.
- **Logistic Regression:** Despite its name, it is used for binary classification tasks.

- **Decision Trees:** A hierarchical model that splits the data based on certain conditions (often used for classification).

- **Support Vector Machines (SVM):** A powerful classifier that finds the optimal boundary (hyperplane) that separates data into different classes.

- **k-Nearest Neighbors (k-NN):** A simple algorithm that classifies new data based on its proximity to labeled data points.

Unsupervised Learning

In unsupervised learning, the algorithm is given data without labels. The goal is to identify hidden patterns or groupings within the data. Since there are no predefined outputs, the model must find structures within the data on its own.

- **Use Cases of Unsupervised Learning:**
  - **Clustering:** Grouping similar data points together. For example, customer segmentation based on purchasing behavior or clustering news articles by topics.

o **Dimensionality Reduction:** Reducing the number of variables in the data while retaining the essential information. This is often used in preprocessing high-dimensional data like images.

Common Algorithms:

- **K-Means Clustering:** A method for partitioning data into K clusters based on similarity.

- **Hierarchical Clustering:** Builds a tree of clusters based on data similarities.

- **Principal Component Analysis (PCA):** A dimensionality reduction technique that transforms data into a lower-dimensional space while preserving as much variance as possible.

Key Differences Between Supervised and Unsupervised Learning:

- **Data:** Supervised learning uses labeled data (input-output pairs), while unsupervised learning uses only input data without labels.

- **Goal:** Supervised learning aims to predict outputs for unseen data, while unsupervised learning seeks to find hidden structures or relationships in data.

- **Examples of Tasks:** Supervised learning is used for tasks like classification and regression; unsupervised learning is used for clustering and dimensionality reduction.

2.3 Introduction to Deep Learning and Neural Networks

What is Deep Learning? Deep learning is a subset of machine learning that focuses on neural networks with many layers (hence the term "deep"). Deep learning models are particularly powerful for tasks such as image recognition, natural language processing, and speech recognition.

At its core, deep learning mimics how the human brain works by using a network of neurons to process data. A neural network consists of layers of interconnected nodes (or "neurons") that transform input data into a prediction or output.

Neural Networks: A neural network consists of layers:

1. **Input Layer:** The first layer that receives the input data.

2. **Hidden Layers:** Layers between the input and output layers that perform various transformations on the data. In deep learning, there are often many hidden layers.

3. **Output Layer:** The final layer that produces the prediction or decision.

Each node in a layer is connected to nodes in the previous and next layers through weights, which are adjusted during training to minimize error in predictions.

Activation Functions: Activation functions determine whether a neuron should be activated (i.e., pass information forward) based on the input it receives. Common activation functions include:

- **Sigmoid:** Maps input values to a range between 0 and 1. Often used for binary classification.

- **ReLU (Rectified Linear Unit):** Introduces non-linearity and helps prevent vanishing gradients, making it popular for deep networks.

- **Tanh:** Similar to sigmoid but maps input to a range between -1 and 1.

- **Softmax:** Often used in the output layer for multi-class classification problems.

How Neural Networks Learn (Backpropagation and Gradient Descent):

- **Backpropagation:** This is the process by which neural networks learn. During training, the model makes predictions and compares them to the actual labels (or target values). The error is propagated back through the network, and the weights are adjusted accordingly.

- **Gradient Descent:** An optimization technique used to minimize the error by adjusting the weights. It calculates the gradient (slope) of the error function and updates the weights in the direction that reduces the error.

Deep Learning Use Cases:

- **Image Recognition:** Convolutional Neural Networks (CNNs) are used to recognize objects in images, such as detecting faces or identifying objects in a photo.

- **Speech Recognition:** Recurrent Neural Networks (RNNs) are used to process sequential data, such as transcribing speech to text.

- **Natural Language Processing (NLP):** Deep learning models, particularly those based on transformers like GPT and BERT, are used to process and understand human language.

- **Machine Learning:** A field of AI that involves creating systems that learn from data. The three main types of learning are supervised, unsupervised, and reinforcement learning.

- **Supervised Learning:** Involves training on labeled data to predict outputs for unseen data. Common algorithms include linear regression, decision trees, and support vector machines.

- **Unsupervised Learning:** Involves finding hidden patterns in unlabeled data. Common techniques include clustering and dimensionality reduction.

- **Deep Learning:** A subset of machine learning that uses neural networks with multiple layers to model complex data. Neural networks, including CNNs and RNNs, are powerful tools for tasks like image recognition and natural language processing.

This chapter introduces the key concepts of machine learning and deep learning, laying the groundwork for the hands-on projects in the following chapters. As we move forward, we'll delve into practical examples using Python and AI libraries to implement these techniques.

CHAPTER 3: SETTING UP YOUR PYTHON ENVIRONMENT FOR AI

Before diving into AI development with Python, it's essential to set up a suitable environment for writing and running your code. This chapter covers everything you need to know to get started with Python for AI, from installing necessary libraries to configuring an integrated development environment (IDE) and using version control to manage your project dependencies.

3.1 Installing Necessary Python Libraries

The first step in setting up your environment is installing the libraries that will enable you to develop AI applications. Below are the core libraries and tools used in AI development.

Step 1: Installing Python

Ensure you have Python installed. If not, you can download and install it from the official Python website: https://www.python.org/downloads/.

For AI development, **Python 3.x** is the recommended version.

Step 2: Setting Up a Virtual Environment

It's a good practice to use a **virtual environment** for each project to avoid conflicts between different Python libraries. Virtual environments isolate dependencies for each project, so one project's dependencies won't interfere with another's.

1. Open a terminal or command prompt and navigate to your project directory.
2. Create a virtual environment by running:

bash

```
python3 -m venv myenv
```

This will create a directory called myenv where the environment is stored.

3. Activate the environment:

   o On Windows:

   bash

   ```
   .\myenv\Scripts\activate
   ```

   o On macOS/Linux:

   bash

   ```
   source myenv/bin/activate
   ```

When the environment is activated, your terminal prompt will change to show the name of the environment, e.g., (myenv).

Step 3: Installing Libraries

Once the virtual environment is set up and activated, you can install the necessary libraries for AI development. For machine learning and deep learning, these are the essential libraries:

1. **NumPy:** For numerical computing.

   bash

```
pip install numpy
```

2. **Pandas:** For data manipulation and analysis.

bash

```
pip install pandas
```

3. **Matplotlib & Seaborn:** For data visualization.

bash

```
pip install matplotlib seaborn
```

4. **Scikit-learn:** For traditional machine learning algorithms.

bash

```
pip install scikit-learn
```

5. **TensorFlow or PyTorch:** For deep learning.

   o   For TensorFlow:

   bash

pip install tensorflow

- o For PyTorch (use the command provided on PyTorch's official site for your specific system configuration):

bash

pip install torch torchvision torchaudio

6. **Jupyter Notebook:** For an interactive coding environment.

bash

pip install jupyter

Step 4: Verifying Installations

Once you've installed the necessary libraries, you can verify their installation by running:

python

import numpy as np

```
import pandas as pd

import matplotlib.pyplot as plt

import seaborn as sns

import tensorflow as tf

import torch
```

If there are no errors, the libraries are correctly installed.

3.2 Setting Up IDEs and Jupyter Notebooks

Choosing an Integrated Development Environment (IDE)

While you can use any text editor to write Python code, an IDE offers features like syntax highlighting, code completion, debugging, and project management. Here are some popular IDEs for Python development:

1. **PyCharm:** A powerful, feature-rich IDE specifically designed for Python. It provides intelligent code assistance, debugging, and integration with version control systems like Git.

   o Download PyCharm

2. **Visual Studio Code (VS Code):** A lightweight, open-source editor with Python support. It's highly customizable and has a wide range of extensions, making it a popular choice for Python development.

   o Download VS Code

3. **Jupyter Notebooks:** Jupyter is an interactive development environment that allows you to write and execute code in cells. It's perfect for data analysis, exploration, and visualizing results step-by-step.

   o To launch Jupyter Notebooks, simply run:

   bash

   jupyter notebook

4. This will open a browser window where you can create and run .ipynb files.

Setting Up Jupyter Notebooks

Jupyter Notebooks are particularly useful in AI and data science because they allow you to:

- Write and execute code in chunks (cells)

- Visualize data directly in the notebook

- Include markdown for documentation and explanations

Once Jupyter is installed, you can launch a new notebook from the terminal:

bash

jupyter notebook

This will open Jupyter in your default browser, where you can create a new Python notebook by selecting "New" -> "Python 3".

Using Jupyter:

- **Cells:** Jupyter notebooks consist of cells. You can run Python code or write markdown to explain your code.

- **Markdown:** Use markdown to annotate your code with explanations, formulas, and images.

- **Execution:** Run a code cell by pressing Shift + Enter. The output will be displayed directly below the cell.

Tip: Save your work often. Notebooks can be saved as .ipynb files.

3.3 Version Control and Managing Dependencies

When working on AI projects, especially if you're collaborating with others or managing large codebases, version control is crucial. It helps you track changes to your code, revert to previous versions, and collaborate efficiently.

Git for Version Control

1. **Install Git:** First, you need to install Git. You can download it from https://git-scm.com/downloads.

2. **Setting up a Git Repository:**

   o Initialize a Git repository in your project directory:

   bash

   git init

   o Stage changes to be committed:

bash

git add .

◦   Commit the changes:

bash

git commit -m "Initial commit"

3. **Using GitHub:** GitHub is a popular platform for hosting Git repositories. Once you've created a repository on GitHub, you can link it to your local repository:

bash

git remote add origin https://github.com/yourusername/yourrepo.git
git push -u origin master

Managing Dependencies with requirements.txt

As you install various libraries and tools, it's essential to track them in a file called requirements.txt. This file lists all the dependencies your project needs to run.

1. To generate requirements.txt with all the installed libraries, run:

bash

pip freeze > requirements.txt

2. If someone else needs to replicate your environment, they can install all the dependencies with:

bash

pip install -r requirements.txt

This ensures that the project can be easily set up on any system with the correct dependencies.

3.4 Managing Environments with conda (Optional)

While pip and virtual environments work well, **Anaconda** is another option that simplifies package management and environment handling, especially for data science and AI projects.

1. **Install**   **Anaconda**   from https://www.anaconda.com/products/individual.

2. Create a new environment with:

bash

```
conda create --name myenv python=3.8
```

3. Activate the environment:

bash

```
conda activate myenv
```

With Anaconda, you can manage Python libraries, versions, and environments all in one place, and it comes with popular libraries like **NumPy**, **Pandas**, and **Scikit-learn** pre-installed.

- **Installing Python Libraries:** Using pip to install essential libraries for AI development such as NumPy, Pandas, TensorFlow, and Scikit-learn.

- **Setting Up IDEs and Jupyter Notebooks:** Configuring development environments like PyCharm, Visual Studio Code, and Jupyter for interactive AI development.

- **Version Control and Dependency Management:** Using Git for version control and requirements.txt to track project dependencies. Anaconda can also be used for managing environments and libraries.

By the end of this chapter, you'll be ready to start building AI applications with Python, equipped with the necessary tools and environment to develop, test, and manage your projects effectively.

CHAPTER 4: WORKING WITH DATA

Data is at the heart of every AI application. For AI models to learn effectively, the data they are trained on must be clean, well-organized, and relevant. In this chapter, we will focus on how to collect, clean, and explore data. We'll also cover how to visualize the data to gain insights before using it for machine learning tasks.

4.1 Data Collection and Cleaning

Data Collection

Before you can work with data, you need to gather it. Data can come from many sources, and it's essential to understand where the data is coming from and how to acquire it. Some common sources of data include:

- **Public datasets:** Websites like Kaggle, UCI Machine Learning Repository, and government open data portals offer a wide variety of datasets in various domains (e.g., healthcare, finance, social media).

- **Web scraping:** If data is available on websites but not in downloadable formats, web scraping tools like **BeautifulSoup** and **Scrapy** can be used to extract data.

- **APIs:** Many platforms, including Twitter, Google, and various financial and news services, provide APIs that allow you to access structured data programmatically.

Example: To get data from Kaggle, you can use the Kaggle API. First, install the Kaggle API using:

bash

```
pip install kaggle
```

Then use the following command to download datasets:

bash

```
kaggle datasets download -d [dataset-name]
```

Data Cleaning

Raw data is rarely in a state that's immediately ready for analysis. **Data cleaning** involves preparing and transforming raw data into a clean, usable format.

Steps for cleaning data:

1. **Remove duplicates:** Sometimes, datasets contain repeated rows. This can skew analysis and model performance.

   python

   ```
   df.drop_duplicates(inplace=True)
   ```

2. **Handle missing values:** Missing values are common in real-world datasets. You can either drop the rows containing missing data or fill them using imputation techniques.

   o Dropping rows with missing values:

   python

   ```
   df.dropna(inplace=True)
   ```

- Imputing missing values (e.g., using the mean for numerical columns):

python

```
df['column_name'].fillna(df['column_name'].mean(),
inplace=True)
```

3. **Fix inconsistent data types:** Sometimes, columns might be misrepresented as the wrong data types (e.g., numeric columns read as strings). You can convert them into the correct types.

python

```
df['column_name'] = pd.to_numeric(df['column_name'], errors='coerce')
```

4. **Remove irrelevant features:** Not all columns in your dataset may be useful for your analysis or modeling. Drop columns that aren't necessary.

python

```
df.drop(['column1', 'column2'], axis=1, inplace=True)
```

5. **Normalize/scale data:** Certain algorithms require numerical data to be on the same scale. You can use techniques like **Min-Max scaling** or **Z-score normalization** to scale your data.

python

```
from sklearn.preprocessing import MinMaxScaler
scaler = MinMaxScaler()
df['scaled_column'] = scaler.fit_transform(df[['column_name']])
```

4.2 Exploratory Data Analysis (EDA)

What is Exploratory Data Analysis (EDA)?

EDA is the process of analyzing data sets to summarize their main characteristics, often using visual methods. It's a crucial step in any data science or AI project because it helps you understand the distribution of variables, identify patterns, spot outliers, and uncover relationships between features. The goal of EDA is to better understand the data and uncover any insights that may guide model selection and preprocessing.

Steps in EDA:

1. **Understand the structure of the data:** Start by inspecting the first few rows and the summary statistics of your dataset.

   python

   ```
   df.head()  # Show first 5 rows
   df.info()  # Get information about the dataset (e.g., data types, non-null counts)
   df.describe()  # Summary statistics for numerical columns
   ```

2. **Identify missing values and outliers:** Before visualizing, check for missing or extreme values. Use methods like boxplots, histograms, and scatter plots to detect outliers.

   o Visualize missing data:

   python

   ```
   import seaborn as sns
   ```

```
sns.heatmap(df.isnull(), cbar=False, cmap='viridis')
```

    o   Identify outliers using boxplots:

python

```
sns.boxplot(x=df['column_name'])
```

3. **Visualizing the distribution of features:** Understanding the distribution of individual features is essential, especially for selecting the right machine learning model and preprocessing techniques.

    o   Histograms and density plots help visualize the distribution of numerical data:

python

```
sns.histplot(df['column_name'], kde=True)
```

4. **Analyzing relationships between variables:** Visualizing relationships between features helps understand correlations or dependencies between them. This can guide feature

engineering or selecting relevant variables for machine learning models.

- o Scatter plots help visualize relationships between two variables:

python

```
sns.scatterplot(x='feature1', y='feature2', data=df)
```

5. **Correlations:** Use heatmaps to visualize correlations between numeric variables. High correlations between features may require feature selection or dimensionality reduction.

python

```
correlation_matrix = df.corr()
sns.heatmap(correlation_matrix, annot=True, cmap='coolwarm', fmt='.2f')
```

Example: Visualizing Categorical Variables For categorical data, bar plots are useful for comparing the frequency of categories:

python

sns.countplot(x='categorical_column', data=df)

4.3 Visualizing Data (Matplotlib, Seaborn)

Visualization is an essential part of EDA, and it allows you to communicate findings effectively. Python offers two primary libraries for data visualization: **Matplotlib** and **Seaborn**. While **Matplotlib** provides basic plotting functionality, **Seaborn** is built on top of Matplotlib and offers a higher-level interface for creating more sophisticated and aesthetically pleasing plots.

Using Matplotlib

Matplotlib is one of the most widely used libraries for data visualization in Python. Here are some basic plotting examples:

1. **Line Plot**: To plot data points over a continuous range (e.g., time series data):

   python

```python
import matplotlib.pyplot as plt

plt.plot(df['x'], df['y'])

plt.xlabel('X-axis')

plt.ylabel('Y-axis')

plt.title('Line Plot Example')

plt.show()
```

2. **Scatter Plot**: Used to visualize the relationship between two variables:

python

```python
plt.scatter(df['x'], df['y'])

plt.xlabel('X-axis')

plt.ylabel('Y-axis')

plt.title('Scatter Plot Example')

plt.show()
```

3. **Bar Plot**: Ideal for comparing categories:

python

```python
plt.bar(df['category'], df['value'])

plt.xlabel('Category')
```

plt.ylabel('Value')

plt.title('Bar Plot Example')

plt.show()

Using Seaborn

Seaborn builds on Matplotlib by providing more advanced statistical plots with better aesthetics and easier customization.

1. **Pairplot**: This creates a grid of scatter plots for numerical features in the dataset:

   python

   ```
   sns.pairplot(df)
   plt.show()
   ```

2. **Boxplot**: Visualizes the distribution of data and identifies outliers:

   python

   ```
   sns.boxplot(x='category', y='value', data=df)
   plt.show()
   ```

3. **Heatmap**: Ideal for visualizing correlation matrices or missing values:

python

```
sns.heatmap(df.corr(), annot=True, cmap='coolwarm')
plt.show()
```

4. **Violin Plot**: Combines aspects of boxplot and kernel density plot, showing the distribution of the data:

python

```
sns.violinplot(x='category', y='value', data=df)
plt.show()
```

Customizing Plots

Both Matplotlib and Seaborn offer ways to customize plots, such as adding titles, labels, adjusting colors, and modifying axes. For example:

python

```
sns.scatterplot(x='feature1', y='feature2', data=df, color='red')

plt.title('Customized Scatter Plot')

plt.xlabel('Feature 1')

plt.ylabel('Feature 2')

plt.show()
```

- **Data Collection:** Data can come from public datasets, APIs, and web scraping. Gather data from relevant sources for your AI project.

- **Data Cleaning:** Raw data often needs to be cleaned to remove duplicates, handle missing values, and convert data into appropriate formats.

- **Exploratory Data Analysis (EDA):** EDA helps summarize and visualize data, allowing you to uncover patterns, detect outliers, and analyze relationships between variables.

- **Data Visualization:** Use Matplotlib and Seaborn for creating different types of plots (e.g., line, scatter, bar, box, heatmaps) to communicate insights from the data.

By the end of this chapter, you'll have the tools and techniques to clean, explore, and visualize your data effectively, setting you up for more advanced AI tasks in later chapters.

CHAPTER 5: INTRODUCTION TO MACHINE LEARNING ALGORITHMS

Machine learning (ML) is a key component of artificial intelligence (AI) that allows computers to learn from data and make predictions or decisions without being explicitly programmed. In this chapter, we will introduce the most fundamental types of machine learning algorithms: **linear regression**, **classification**, and **clustering**. We will also discuss their real-world applications, such as predicting house prices and customer segmentation.

5.1 Overview of Machine Learning Algorithms

Machine learning algorithms can be broadly classified into **supervised** and **unsupervised** learning algorithms:

- **Supervised learning**: Involves learning from labeled data, where the algorithm is trained on input-output pairs, and the model's goal is to predict the output for new, unseen inputs.

Common supervised learning tasks include **regression** and **classification**.

- **Unsupervised learning**: Involves learning from data that is not labeled. The algorithm tries to find patterns, structures, or clusters within the data. Common unsupervised learning tasks include **clustering** and **dimensionality reduction**.

In this chapter, we will focus on basic supervised algorithms (linear regression and classification) and unsupervised learning (clustering).

5.2 Linear Regression (Supervised Learning)

Linear regression is one of the simplest and most commonly used algorithms in machine learning for predicting a continuous target variable based on one or more input features. It assumes that there is a linear relationship between the input variables (independent variables) and the target variable (dependent variable).

The formula for simple linear regression is:

$y = \beta_0 + \beta_1 x$

Where:

- yyy is the predicted value.

- $\beta0\backslash beta\_0\beta0$ is the intercept (constant term).

- $\beta1\backslash beta\_1\beta1$ is the coefficient (weight) of the feature xxx.

In the case of multiple features (multiple linear regression), the formula becomes:

$$y=\beta0+\beta1x1+\beta2x2+\cdots+\beta nxny = \backslash beta\_0 + \backslash beta\_1 x\_1 + \backslash beta\_2 x\_2 + \backslash dots + \backslash beta\_n x\_ny=\beta0+\beta1x1+\beta2x2+\cdots+\beta nxn$$

Key Steps:

1. **Fitting the Model**: The algorithm finds the best-fit line by minimizing the error (typically measured using **Mean Squared Error** or MSE).

2. **Prediction**: Once the model is trained, it can predict the value of yyy for new data based on the learned coefficients $\beta0,\beta1,\ldots\backslash beta\_0, \backslash beta\_1, \backslash dots\beta0,\beta1,\ldots$.

Example: Predicting House Prices

In a real-world scenario, we might use linear regression to predict the price of a house based on features like square footage, number of bedrooms, location, etc.

Code Example:

python

```
import pandas as pd
from sklearn.linear_model import LinearRegression
from sklearn.model_selection import train_test_split
from sklearn.metrics import mean_squared_error

# Load the dataset
df = pd.read_csv('house_prices.csv')

# Features (X) and target variable (y)
X = df[['square_footage', 'num_bedrooms', 'num_bathrooms']]
y = df['price']

# Split the data into training and testing sets
X_train, X_test, y_train, y_test = train_test_split(X, y, test_size=0.2,
random_state=42)
```

```
# Initialize and train the model

model = LinearRegression()

model.fit(X_train, y_train)


# Predict the house prices

y_pred = model.predict(X_test)


# Evaluate the model using Mean Squared Error (MSE)

mse = mean_squared_error(y_test, y_pred)

print(f'Mean Squared Error: {mse}')
```

Real-World Application:

- In real estate, linear regression can be used to predict house prices based on various features like square footage, location, age of the house, etc.

5.3 Classification (Supervised Learning)

Classification is a type of supervised learning where the goal is to predict a discrete class label (e.g., spam or not spam, disease or no disease) based on input features.

A classification model is trained with labeled data, and it learns to assign an input to one of the predefined categories. **Logistic regression, decision trees**, and **support vector machines (SVMs)** are common classification algorithms.

The output of a classification model is usually a probability score or a class label. For binary classification, the model typically outputs a value between 0 and 1, which is then mapped to a class label (0 or 1).

Example: Predicting Whether a Customer Will Buy a Product

Suppose we want to predict whether a customer will buy a product based on their age, income, and previous purchasing behavior. This is a **binary classification** problem, where the target variable is 1 (purchase) or 0 (no purchase).

Code Example:

python

```python
from sklearn.linear_model import LogisticRegression
from sklearn.model_selection import train_test_split
from sklearn.metrics import accuracy_score

# Load the dataset
df = pd.read_csv('customer_data.csv')

# Features (X) and target variable (y)
X = df[['age', 'income', 'previous_purchases']]
y = df['purchase']

# Split the data into training and testing sets
X_train, X_test, y_train, y_test = train_test_split(X, y, test_size=0.2,
random_state=42)

# Initialize and train the logistic regression model
model = LogisticRegression()
model.fit(X_train, y_train)

# Predict whether customers will purchase the product
y_pred = model.predict(X_test)
```

Evaluate the model's performance

accuracy = accuracy_score(y_test, y_pred)

print(f'Accuracy: {accuracy}')

Real-World Application:

- In marketing, classification models can predict whether a customer will respond to a marketing campaign, which helps businesses target the right audience.

5.4 Clustering (Unsupervised Learning)

Clustering is an unsupervised learning technique that aims to group similar data points together into clusters based on certain characteristics. Unlike classification, clustering does not use labeled data and is typically used to explore the structure of the data.

K-means is one of the most popular clustering algorithms. The basic idea of K-means is to partition the data into KKK clusters, where each data point belongs to the cluster whose mean (centroid) is closest to the point.

Example: Customer Segmentation

In a retail business, clustering can be used to segment customers into distinct groups based on purchasing behavior. These segments can then be targeted with personalized marketing strategies.

Code Example:

python

```
from sklearn.cluster import KMeans
import matplotlib.pyplot as plt

# Load the dataset
df = pd.read_csv('customer_data.csv')

# Features (X)
X = df[['age', 'income', 'previous_purchases']]

# Apply KMeans clustering
kmeans = KMeans(n_clusters=3, random_state=42)
df['cluster'] = kmeans.fit_predict(X)
```

```
# Plotting the clusters

plt.scatter(df['age'], df['income'], c=df['cluster'], cmap='viridis')

plt.xlabel('Age')

plt.ylabel('Income')

plt.title('Customer Segmentation using K-Means')

plt.show()
```

Real-World Application:

- **Customer segmentation**: Retailers can use clustering to group customers into distinct segments based on purchasing habits. These segments can then be targeted with different marketing campaigns to improve sales and customer retention.

- **Market research**: In industries like finance and healthcare, clustering is used to find patterns in customer behavior or identify subgroups with similar characteristics.

- **Linear Regression**: A supervised algorithm for predicting a continuous target variable based on one or more input features. It is commonly used in applications like predicting house prices, sales forecasting, or stock prices.

- **Classification**: A supervised learning algorithm used for predicting discrete labels or categories (e.g., yes/no, spam/not spam). It is used in applications like customer churn prediction, medical diagnosis, and email classification.

- **Clustering**: An unsupervised learning algorithm that groups similar data points into clusters. It is useful in applications like customer segmentation, image compression, and anomaly detection.

By the end of this chapter, you should have a solid understanding of the basic machine learning algorithms: **linear regression**, **classification**, and **clustering**. You will also have practical experience applying these algorithms to real-world examples, such as predicting house prices and segmenting customers.

CHAPTER 6: ADVANCED MACHINE LEARNING TECHNIQUES

In this chapter, we'll explore more advanced machine learning algorithms that are widely used in various industries for more complex predictive tasks. Specifically, we will cover **decision trees**, **random forests**, and **k-nearest neighbors (k-NN)**. Additionally, we will walk through a case study on **building a recommendation system**, a practical application of advanced machine learning techniques in real-world scenarios like e-commerce and content platforms.

6.1 Decision Trees

A **decision tree** is a supervised machine learning algorithm that can be used for both classification and regression tasks. It splits the data into subsets based on the value of input features, creating a tree-like model of decisions. The goal is to divide the dataset into smaller subsets in a way that the target variable becomes increasingly homogeneous within each subset.

How Decision Trees Work:

1. **Root Node**: The first decision point, where the dataset is split based on a feature.

2. **Branches**: Each branch represents a decision based on a feature's value.

3. **Leaf Nodes**: The final decision or prediction, representing the target variable.

Decision trees are built by selecting the feature that best splits the data at each node. The effectiveness of a split is typically measured by metrics like **Gini Impurity** or **Information Gain** (for classification tasks) and **Mean Squared Error (MSE)** (for regression tasks).

Example: Predicting Loan Approval Using Decision Trees

Let's say you're building a model to predict whether a loan will be approved based on factors such as income, credit score, and debt-to-income ratio.

Code Example:

python

```
from sklearn.tree import DecisionTreeClassifier
from sklearn.model_selection import train_test_split
from sklearn.metrics import accuracy_score


# Load dataset
df = pd.read_csv('loan_data.csv')


# Features (X) and target variable (y)
X = df[['income', 'credit_score', 'debt_to_income']]
y = df['loan_approval']


# Split the data into training and testing sets
X_train, X_test, y_train, y_test = train_test_split(X, y, test_size=0.2,
random_state=42)
```

```
# Initialize and train the decision tree classifier

dt_model = DecisionTreeClassifier(random_state=42)

dt_model.fit(X_train, y_train)


# Make predictions

y_pred = dt_model.predict(X_test)


# Evaluate the model's performance

accuracy = accuracy_score(y_test, y_pred)

print(f'Accuracy: {accuracy}')
```

Advantages of Decision Trees:

- **Interpretability**: Easy to visualize and interpret the decisions being made.
- **Handles Non-linear Relationships**: Can capture complex relationships between features.

Disadvantages:

- **Overfitting**: Decision trees can easily overfit, especially if they are too deep (complex).

- **Instability**: Small changes in data can lead to different tree structures.

6.2 Random Forests

A **random forest** is an ensemble method that combines multiple decision trees to improve predictive performance and reduce overfitting. It works by constructing many decision trees during training and outputting the average prediction (for regression) or the mode (for classification) of all individual trees.

Each tree in a random forest is trained on a random subset of the data (using bootstrapping), and only a random subset of features is considered when splitting each node, which introduces diversity into the model.

Why Random Forests Are Effective:

- **Reduced Overfitting**: By averaging predictions from many trees, random forests reduce the risk of overfitting compared to a single decision tree.

- **High Accuracy**: Random forests often outperform individual decision trees in terms of accuracy.

Example: Predicting Customer Churn Using Random Forests

In a customer churn prediction problem, you can use a random forest classifier to predict whether a customer will leave based on features like usage patterns, subscription type, and customer service interactions.

Code Example:

python

```
from sklearn.ensemble import RandomForestClassifier
from sklearn.model_selection import train_test_split
from sklearn.metrics import accuracy_score

# Load dataset
df = pd.read_csv('customer_churn.csv')

# Features (X) and target variable (y)
X = df[['usage', 'subscription_type', 'customer_service_calls']]
```

```python
y = df['churn']


# Split the data into training and testing sets
X_train, X_test, y_train, y_test = train_test_split(X, y, test_size=0.2,
random_state=42)


# Initialize and train the random forest classifier
rf_model = RandomForestClassifier(n_estimators=100, random_state=42)
rf_model.fit(X_train, y_train)


# Make predictions
y_pred = rf_model.predict(X_test)


# Evaluate the model's performance
accuracy = accuracy_score(y_test, y_pred)
print(f'Accuracy: {accuracy}')
```

Advantages of Random Forests:

- **Less Prone to Overfitting**: The randomness in feature selection and bootstrapping helps to prevent overfitting.

- **Robust to Noise**: Random forests handle noisy data and outliers better than a single decision tree.

Disadvantages:

- **Model Interpretability**: While individual decision trees are easy to interpret, a random forest is harder to explain due to the ensemble of trees.

- **Computationally Intensive**: Random forests require more computational resources, especially with large datasets.

6.3 k-Nearest Neighbors (k-NN)

The **k-nearest neighbors (k-NN)** algorithm is a simple, instance-based, supervised learning algorithm. The idea behind k-NN is that the prediction for a new data point is based on the majority label (for classification) or average label (for regression) of its **k** nearest neighbors in the feature space.

How k-NN Works:

1. Choose the number of neighbors, **k**.

2. Compute the distance between the new data point and all other data points in the training set (using distance metrics like Euclidean distance).

3. Sort the data points by distance.

4. Assign the label based on the majority class of the **k** nearest neighbors.

Example: Classifying Iris Species Using k-NN

The **Iris dataset** is a well-known dataset used for classification tasks, where we classify iris flowers into one of three species based on their features (sepal length, sepal width, petal length, and petal width).

Code Example:

python

```
from sklearn.neighbors import KNeighborsClassifier
from sklearn.model_selection import train_test_split
from sklearn.metrics import accuracy_score
from sklearn.datasets import load_iris
```

```
# Load the iris dataset
iris = load_iris()
X = iris.data.
y = iris.target


# Split the data into training and testing sets
X_train, X_test, y_train, y_test = train_test_split(X, y, test_size=0.2,
random_state=42)


# Initialize and train the k-NN classifier
knn_model = KNeighborsClassifier(n_neighbors=3)
knn_model.fit(X_train, y_train)


# Make predictions
y_pred = knn_model.predict(X_test)


# Evaluate the model's performance
accuracy = accuracy_score(y_test, y_pred)
print(f'Accuracy: {accuracy}')
```

Advantages of k-NN:

- **Simple and Intuitive**: Easy to understand and implement.

- **No Training Phase**: Since k-NN is an instance-based algorithm, it doesn't require a training phase; it just stores the data.

Disadvantages:

- **Computationally Expensive**: For large datasets, k-NN can be slow since it needs to compute distances for each query point.
- **Sensitive to Feature Scaling**: k-NN is sensitive to the scale of the data, so feature scaling (e.g., normalization) is crucial.

6.4 Case Study: Building a Recommendation System

A **recommendation system** is an application of machine learning that suggests products, content, or services to users based on various factors, such as their past behavior, preferences, and the behavior of similar users.

Recommendation systems are widely used in platforms like **Amazon**, **Netflix**, and **Spotify**. There are two main types of recommendation systems:

- **Collaborative Filtering**: Makes predictions based on the preferences of similar users.
- **Content-Based Filtering**: Makes predictions based on the features of items and user preferences.

In this case study, we will build a simple **collaborative filtering** recommendation system using **k-NN** to recommend movies based on users' movie ratings.

Steps:

1. **Load the Dataset**: The MovieLens dataset is commonly used for recommendation systems.
2. **Preprocess the Data**: Format the dataset into a matrix where rows represent users and columns represent movies, with ratings as the values.

3. **Use k-NN**: For each user, find the k-nearest users based on similarity (e.g., cosine similarity) and recommend movies that those similar users have rated highly.

Code Example:

python

```
import pandas as pd
from sklearn.neighbors import NearestNeighbors
from sklearn.metrics.pairwise import cosine_similarity

# Load MovieLens dataset (user-item ratings matrix)
df = pd.read_csv('ratings.csv')  # This is a user-item rating matrix

# Create a pivot table with users as rows and movies as columns
user_movie_matrix = df.pivot_table(index='userId', columns='movieId', values='rating')

# Fill missing ratings with 0 (for simplicity, though other imputation techniques exist)
user_movie_matrix.fillna(0, inplace=True)
```

```
# Calculate cosine similarity between users

cosine_sim = cosine_similarity(user_movie_matrix)


# Use NearestNeighbors for collaborative filtering

knn = NearestNeighbors(n_neighbors=5, metric='cosine')

knn.fit(user_movie_matrix)


# Find the k nearest neighbors for a given user

user_id = 1  # Example user

distances, indices = knn.kneighbors(user_movie_matrix.iloc[user_id - 1,
:].values.reshape(1, -1))


# Recommend movies based on the nearest neighbors

recommended_movies           =           user_movie_matrix.iloc[indices[0],
:].mean(axis=0).sort_values(ascending=False).head(5)

print(recommended_movies)
```

Real-World Application:

- **E-commerce**: Platforms like Amazon use recommendation systems to suggest products based on past purchases, ratings, and the behavior of similar users.

- **Streaming Services**: Netflix and Spotify recommend movies, TV shows, and music based on users' previous preferences and ratings.

- **Decision Trees**: A simple, interpretable algorithm for classification and regression, but prone to overfitting.

- **Random Forests**: An ensemble method that combines multiple decision trees, reducing overfitting and increasing accuracy.

- **k-NN**: A non-parametric, instance-based learning algorithm used for classification and regression, ideal for problems where relationships between data points are complex.

- **Recommendation Systems**: Uses collaborative filtering or content-based filtering to suggest relevant items to users based on their preferences and similar users' behavior.

By the end of this chapter, you should be comfortable with using decision trees, random forests, and k-NN for a range of machine learning problems, and you should have gained hands-on experience building a recommendation system using collaborative filtering techniques.

CHAPTER 7: NEURAL NETWORKS AND DEEP LEARNING

In this chapter, we will dive into **neural networks** and **deep learning**, two of the most powerful tools in modern AI. Neural networks are the foundation of many cutting-edge AI applications, from image recognition to natural language processing. We will cover the basic structure of neural networks, the key concepts behind **activation functions** and **backpropagation**, and then apply them to a **real-world example** of **image classification** using **Convolutional Neural Networks (CNNs)**.

7.1 Introduction to Neural Networks

A **neural network** is a type of machine learning model inspired by the human brain's network of neurons. It consists of layers of **artificial neurons** (also called **nodes**), where each neuron receives input, processes it using an activation function, and passes the output to subsequent layers. Neural networks are designed to recognize patterns and can learn from data to perform tasks such as classification, regression, and clustering.

Basic Structure of a Neural Network:

1. **Input Layer**: This layer receives the input features (e.g., pixels of an image, numerical data points). Each input node corresponds to one feature.

2. **Hidden Layers**: These are intermediate layers between the input and output layers. The network learns complex representations of the input data through multiple hidden layers.

3. **Output Layer**: This layer produces the model's final prediction. For a classification task, this could represent the different classes, while for regression, it would produce a continuous value.

The most basic type of neural network is the **feedforward neural network** (FNN), where the data moves in one direction from input to output without any cycles.

7.2 Activation Functions and Backpropagation

Activation functions and **backpropagation** are two key concepts that make neural networks capable of learning from data.

7.2.1 Activation Functions

An **activation function** determines the output of a neuron based on the input it receives. Without activation functions, a neural network would essentially be just a linear regression model, as all the layers would be reducible to a linear transformation.

Common activation functions include:

- **Sigmoid Function**: Produces an output between 0 and 1, making it suitable for binary classification tasks.

  $\sigma(x) = \frac{1}{1 + e^{-x}}$

- **ReLU (Rectified Linear Unit)**: The most widely used activation function in modern neural networks. It outputs the input directly if it's positive; otherwise, it outputs zero.

ReLU(x)=max⌊fo⌉(0,x)\text{ReLU}(x)   =   \max(0,

x)ReLU(x)=max(0,x)

- **Tanh**: Similar to sigmoid but outputs values between -1 and 1. Often used in hidden layers.

Tanh(x)=21+e−2x−1\text{Tanh}(x) = \frac{2}{1 + e^{-2x}}

- 1Tanh(x)=1+e−2x2−1

- **Softmax**: Typically used in the output layer of classification tasks with multiple classes. It converts logits (raw predictions) into probabilities.

Softmax(xi)=exi∑j=1nexj\text{Softmax}(x_i)   =

\frac{e^{x_i}}{\sum_{j=1}^n e^{x_j}}Softmax(xi)=∑j=1n

exjexi

7.2.2 Backpropagation

Backpropagation is the process by which neural networks learn. It is an optimization algorithm used to minimize the error (or loss) of a network by adjusting the weights of the neurons. Backpropagation works through the following steps:

1. **Forward Pass**: The input is passed through the network, layer by layer, to produce the final output (predictions).

2. **Loss Calculation**: The loss function (e.g., mean squared error or cross-entropy) measures the difference between the predicted output and the true output.

3. **Backward Pass**: Backpropagation calculates the gradient of the loss function with respect to each weight in the network, starting from the output layer and moving backward through the hidden layers.

4. **Weight Update**: The weights are updated using an optimization algorithm, usually **Gradient Descent**, which adjusts the weights in the direction that reduces the error.

The key idea is that by iteratively adjusting the weights in response to errors, the neural network can learn to make better predictions.

7.3 Real-World Use: Image Classification with CNNs

One of the most powerful applications of neural networks is **image classification**. In this section, we will introduce **Convolutional Neural Networks (CNNs)**, a specialized type of neural network designed for analyzing visual data.

7.3.1 What is a Convolutional Neural Network (CNN)?

A **Convolutional Neural Network (CNN)** is a type of deep neural network specifically designed for image data. Unlike traditional fully connected networks, CNNs use convolutional layers that apply filters (kernels) to local patches of the input image to extract features such as edges, textures, and shapes.

The architecture of a CNN typically consists of the following layers:

1. **Convolutional Layer**: This layer applies multiple filters to the input image to extract spatial features. Each filter detects specific patterns such as edges or corners.

2. **Activation Layer**: Typically, a ReLU activation function is applied after the convolutional layer to introduce non-linearity.

3. **Pooling Layer**: This layer reduces the spatial dimensions of the image (downsampling) while retaining important features, typically using **max pooling** or **average pooling**.

4. **Fully Connected Layer**: After several convolutional and pooling layers, the network typically has one or more fully connected layers to combine the features and make predictions.

5. **Output Layer**: The final layer produces the predicted class labels, usually with a **Softmax** activation function for multi-class classification tasks.

7.3.2 Building a Simple CNN for Image Classification

Let's walk through an example of how to build a simple CNN for classifying images using the **Keras** library with **TensorFlow** backend. We'll use the **CIFAR-10** dataset, which consists of 60,000 32x32 color images in 10 classes, such as airplanes, cars, and birds.

Code Example:

python

```
import tensorflow as tf

from tensorflow.keras import layers, models

from tensorflow.keras.datasets import cifar10

from tensorflow.keras.utils import to_categorical


# Load and preprocess the CIFAR-10 dataset
(X_train, y_train), (X_test, y_test) = cifar10.load_data()
X_train, X_test = X_train / 255.0, X_test / 255.0  # Normalize images to [0, 1]
y_train, y_test = to_categorical(y_train, 10), to_categorical(y_test, 10)  # One-hot
encode labels


# Build the CNN model
model = models.Sequential([
    layers.Conv2D(32, (3, 3), activation='relu', input_shape=(32, 32, 3)),  #
Convolutional layer
    layers.MaxPooling2D((2, 2)),  # Pooling layer
    layers.Conv2D(64, (3, 3), activation='relu'),  # Second convolutional layer
    layers.MaxPooling2D((2, 2)),  # Pooling layer
    layers.Conv2D(64, (3, 3), activation='relu'),  # Third convolutional layer
    layers.Flatten(),  # Flatten the 3D data into 1D
    layers.Dense(64, activation='relu'),  # Fully connected layer
    layers.Dense(10, activation='softmax')  # Output layer with softmax activation
])
```

```
# Compile the model
model.compile(optimizer='adam',
        loss='categorical_crossentropy',
        metrics=['accuracy'])

# Train the model
model.fit(X_train, y_train, epochs=10, validation_data=(X_test, y_test))

# Evaluate the model on test data
test_loss, test_acc = model.evaluate(X_test, y_test)
print(f'Test accuracy: {test_acc}')
```

Explanation of the Model:

- **Convolutional Layers**: Extracts features from images by applying multiple filters.
- **Max Pooling Layers**: Reduces the dimensionality of the feature maps, improving computational efficiency.
- **Fully Connected Layer**: After feature extraction, the dense layer combines features to predict the output.

- **Softmax Activation**: The final layer uses softmax to output the probabilities for each of the 10 classes.

Real-World Applications:

- **Image Recognition**: CNNs are the backbone of modern image classification systems. They power applications such as facial recognition, self-driving cars, and medical image analysis (e.g., detecting tumors in X-rays).

- **Object Detection**: CNNs can be extended to object detection, identifying and locating objects within an image, which is crucial for applications like video surveillance or autonomous robots.

- **Video Processing**: CNNs can also be applied to video frames for tasks like activity recognition, motion tracking, or event detection.

- **Neural Networks**: Inspired by the human brain, neural networks learn complex patterns from data through layers of interconnected neurons.

- **Activation Functions**: Functions like ReLU and Sigmoid introduce non-linearity into the network, allowing it to learn complex patterns.

- **Backpropagation**: The algorithm that allows neural networks to learn by adjusting weights based on errors (gradients).

- **CNNs**: A special type of neural network designed for processing image data, with layers like convolutional layers, pooling layers, and fully connected layers.

- **Image Classification**: Using CNNs for classifying images in tasks like object recognition, face detection, and medical image analysis.

By the end of this chapter, you should have a solid understanding of how neural networks and deep learning work, how activation functions and backpropagation enable learning, and how to build and train a CNN for image classification.

CHAPTER 8: WORKING WITH NATURAL LANGUAGE PROCESSING (NLP)

In this chapter, we will explore **Natural Language Processing (NLP)**, a crucial subfield of artificial intelligence that focuses on enabling computers to understand, interpret, and generate human language. NLP is used in a wide range of applications, from chatbots and virtual assistants to sentiment analysis and language translation.

We will cover:

1. **Text Preprocessing and Tokenization**: Essential steps to prepare raw text data for NLP tasks.

2. **Sentiment Analysis**: A popular NLP application where we determine the sentiment (positive, negative, or neutral) of a given piece of text.

3. **Case Study: Chatbots and Language Models**: How advanced NLP models like **GPT** and **BERT** power

conversational agents and other language-related applications.

8.1 Text Preprocessing and Tokenization

Text preprocessing is a critical step in preparing raw text for machine learning tasks. Raw text is messy—sometimes noisy, full of irrelevant characters, punctuation, and stopwords that do not contribute meaningfully to the model's performance. Preprocessing transforms this raw text into a structured format suitable for analysis.

8.1.1 Key Text Preprocessing Steps

- **Lowercasing**: Converting all characters to lowercase to ensure uniformity.

  Example: "The Quick Brown Fox" becomes "the quick brown fox".

- **Removing Punctuation**: Punctuation marks do not carry meaningful information for most NLP tasks.

Example: "Hello, world!" becomes "Hello world".

- **Removing Stopwords**: Stopwords like "the", "a", and "is" are often removed as they don't contribute much to the meaning.

- **Stemming**: Reducing words to their root form (e.g., "running" becomes "run").

- **Lemmatization**: Similar to stemming but more advanced, lemmatization uses vocabulary and grammatical knowledge to reduce words to their base form (e.g., "better" becomes "good").

8.1.2 Tokenization

Tokenization is the process of splitting text into individual words or subwords. Tokenization is often one of the first steps in NLP, as it breaks down text into manageable units for further processing.

There are two common approaches:

1. **Word Tokenization**: Splitting text into words.

2. **Sentence Tokenization**: Splitting text into sentences.

Example of Tokenization:

python

```
from nltk.tokenize import word_tokenize

text = "I love programming with Python!"
tokens = word_tokenize(text)
print(tokens)
```

Output:

css

```
['I', 'love', 'programming', 'with', 'Python', '!']
```

For more complex tasks, such as in **transformers** (like BERT or GPT), tokenization can involve breaking words into subword units (using methods like **Byte Pair Encoding (BPE)**), which allows the model to handle out-of-vocabulary words more effectively.

8.2 Sentiment Analysis Using Python

Sentiment analysis is the task of determining the emotional tone (positive, negative, neutral) behind a text. It's commonly used in analyzing customer reviews, social media posts, and feedback. We will use **TextBlob**, a simple NLP library in Python, to perform sentiment analysis.

8.2.1 Using TextBlob for Sentiment Analysis

TextBlob provides an easy-to-use API for NLP tasks like part-of-speech tagging, noun phrase extraction, translation, and, of course, sentiment analysis. It assigns a sentiment polarity score to a text, ranging from -1 (negative sentiment) to +1 (positive sentiment). It also assigns a subjectivity score ranging from 0 to 1 (0 being objective, 1 being subjective).

Code Example: Sentiment Analysis with TextBlob:

python

```
from textblob import TextBlob

# Example text
text = "I absolutely love this product! It's amazing."
```

```python
# Create a TextBlob object

blob = TextBlob(text)


# Get sentiment polarity

polarity = blob.sentiment.polarity

subjectivity = blob.sentiment.subjectivity


# Display results

print(f"Sentiment Polarity: {polarity}")

print(f"Sentiment Subjectivity: {subjectivity}")
```

Output:

yaml

Sentiment Polarity: 0.75

Sentiment Subjectivity: 0.9

A **polarity score** of 0.75 indicates a positive sentiment, while the **subjectivity score** of 0.9 shows that the text is highly subjective.

8.2.2 Using VADER for Sentiment Analysis

For more nuanced sentiment analysis, particularly with social media data, **VADER (Valence Aware Dictionary and sEntiment**

Reasoner) is an excellent tool. VADER is optimized for social media text and works well with emoticons, slangs, and abbreviations.

Code Example: Sentiment Analysis with VADER:

python

```
from nltk.sentiment import SentimentIntensityAnalyzer
```

```
# Example text
text = "I'm so excited about the new release! #BestDayEver"
```

```
# Initialize VADER sentiment analyzer
sia = SentimentIntensityAnalyzer()
```

```
# Get sentiment scores
scores = sia.polarity_scores(text)
```

```
# Display results
print(scores)
```

Output:

arduino

{'neg': 0.0, 'neu': 0.364, 'pos': 0.636, 'compound': 0.896}

The **compound score** is a normalized score that aggregates the positive, neutral, and negative scores into one number. A score above 0.05 typically indicates positive sentiment, while a score below -0.05 indicates negative sentiment.

8.3 Case Study: Chatbots and Language Models

Chatbots and **language models** have become essential in many applications, from customer service to personal assistants. These models are built on large neural networks trained to understand and generate human-like responses. We will explore how **sequence-to-sequence models**, **transformers**, and **pre-trained language models** like **GPT** and **BERT** enable chatbots to function effectively.

8.3.1 Building a Simple Chatbot with Python

A **chatbot** can be a rule-based system (where responses are predefined) or a data-driven system (where responses are generated based on the user's input). Here, we'll build a basic rule-based chatbot using **NLTK** to process inputs and provide responses.

Code Example: Simple Rule-Based Chatbot:

python

```python
import nltk
from nltk.chat.util import Chat, reflections

# Define pairs of user input and bot response
pairs = [
    (r"Hi|Hello|Hey", ["Hello, how can I help you today?"]),
    (r"How are you?", ["I'm doing great, thank you for asking!"]),
    (r"(.*)(weather|today)(.*)", ["The weather is great today!"]),
    (r"quit", ["Goodbye! Have a nice day!"])
]

# Create a chatbot using the defined pairs
chatbot = Chat(pairs, reflections)

# Start the chatbot
chatbot.converse()
```

This simple chatbot uses predefined patterns (regular expressions) to match user inputs and provide responses. However, for more advanced chatbots, we use **sequence-to-sequence models** or

transformers to generate responses dynamically based on the conversation history.

8.3.2 Using Pre-Trained Models for Conversational AI

To create more intelligent chatbots, we can use **pre-trained language models** like **GPT-3** or **BERT**. These models are fine-tuned on vast amounts of text data and can generate coherent, context-aware responses.

Here, we'll look at how to interact with **Hugging Face's Transformers library**, which provides easy access to pre-trained models for various NLP tasks, including question answering, translation, and text generation.

Code Example: Using GPT-2 for Text Generation:

```python
from transformers import GPT2LMHeadModel, GPT2Tokenizer

# Load the pre-trained GPT-2 model and tokenizer
model = GPT2LMHeadModel.from_pretrained("gpt2")
tokenizer = GPT2Tokenizer.from_pretrained("gpt2")
```

```
# Encode the input text

input_text = "What is the future of artificial intelligence?"

inputs = tokenizer.encode(input_text, return_tensors="pt")


# Generate a response

output = model.generate(inputs, max_length=100, num_return_sequences=1,
no_repeat_ngram_size=2)


# Decode and display the output

response = tokenizer.decode(output[0], skip_special_tokens=True)

print(response)
```

Output:

vbnet

What is the future of artificial intelligence? In the future, AI will be able to think and reason on its own, without the need for human intervention. It will be able to perform tasks that are currently impossible for humans, such as understanding complex concepts, creating art, and solving global problems.

8.3.3 Applications of Chatbots and Language Models

- **Customer Support**: Chatbots like those used by companies (e.g., Zendesk, Intercom) handle customer inquiries, resolve issues, and provide instant assistance, reducing the need for human intervention.

- **Personal Assistants**: Virtual assistants such as **Siri**, **Alexa**, and **Google Assistant** use NLP to interact with users, answer questions, and control smart devices.

- **Mental Health**: Chatbots like **Woebot** provide cognitive behavioral therapy (CBT) and offer mental health support through text-based conversations.

- **Text Preprocessing**: Essential steps to clean and format raw text data for analysis, including tokenization, stemming, and removing stopwords.

- **Sentiment Analysis**: A technique for analyzing text to determine the emotional tone behind it (positive, negative, or neutral).

- **Chatbots and Language Models**: Built using **NLP models** such as **sequence-to-sequence** and **transformers** (like GPT and BERT), these models enable machines to understand and generate human-like language.

By the end of this chapter, you should have a good understanding of how to preprocess text, perform sentiment analysis, and build simple chatbots, as well as gain insight into the advanced language models powering modern conversational AI.

CHAPTER 9: BUILDING AI MODELS WITH SCIKIT-LEARN

In this chapter, we will walk through the process of building machine learning models using **Scikit-learn**, one of the most popular libraries for machine learning in Python. We'll go through the end-to-end workflow, from data preparation and feature engineering to training and evaluating models. Finally, we'll apply these concepts in a **real-world case study**—building a **fraud detection system**.

9.1 End-to-End Workflow of Building a Machine Learning Model

The process of building a machine learning model can be broken down into several stages. Each stage is important, and skipping any of them can lead to poor model performance or errors in your analysis. Below is the typical workflow for building a machine learning model in Scikit-learn:

9.1.1 Step 1: Data Collection

The first step in building any machine learning model is to collect the data that will be used to train and test the model. This could involve obtaining a dataset from an existing source (like Kaggle, UCI Machine Learning Repository, or a company database) or collecting data manually.

Example: For a fraud detection system, you would collect historical transaction data that includes features such as transaction amount, user ID, transaction type, and whether the transaction was fraudulent.

9.1.2 Step 2: Data Preprocessing and Cleaning

Once the data is collected, it often needs to be cleaned and prepared for use. This stage can include:

- **Handling Missing Data**: Missing values should be addressed through imputation or removal.

- **Data Transformation**: Scaling numerical features (e.g., using StandardScaler or MinMaxScaler) or encoding categorical variables (e.g., using OneHotEncoder).

- **Removing Outliers**: Identifying and removing outliers that could skew the results.

- **Feature Engineering**: Creating new features based on domain knowledge or existing ones.

9.1.3 Step 3: Splitting the Data into Training and Testing Sets

In this step, we divide the data into a **training set** and a **test set**. The training set is used to train the model, while the test set is used to evaluate its performance. Typically, a split of 80% training and 20% testing is common.

python

```
from sklearn.model_selection import train_test_split

# Split data into training and testing sets (80/20 split)
X_train, X_test, y_train, y_test = train_test_split(X, y, test_size=0.2, random_state=42)
```

9.1.4 Step 4: Choosing a Machine Learning Model

This step involves selecting the appropriate machine learning model based on the problem at hand. For a classification problem like fraud detection, common models include **Logistic Regression**, **Random Forest**, **Support Vector Machines (SVM)**, and **Gradient Boosting**.

Scikit-learn provides a variety of models to choose from, each with its own strengths depending on the problem and data.

9.1.5 Step 5: Training the Model

Once you've selected a model, the next step is to **train** it on the training data. This is done using the .fit() method in Scikit-learn.

python

```
from sklearn.ensemble import RandomForestClassifier

# Initialize and train the model
model = RandomForestClassifier()
model.fit(X_train, y_train)
```

9.1.6 Step 6: Evaluating the Model

After training, we need to evaluate the model's performance on the test set to determine how well it generalizes to unseen data. Common evaluation metrics for classification problems include:

- **Accuracy**: The proportion of correct predictions.
- **Precision**: The proportion of positive predictions that are actually correct.

- **Recall**: The proportion of actual positives that are correctly identified.

- **F1-Score**: The harmonic mean of precision and recall, useful for imbalanced classes.

- **ROC-AUC**: The area under the Receiver Operating Characteristic curve, especially important for binary classification tasks.

python

```
from sklearn.metrics import classification_report, confusion_matrix

# Evaluate the model
y_pred = model.predict(X_test)
print(classification_report(y_test, y_pred))
print(confusion_matrix(y_test, y_pred))
```

9.1.7 Step 7: Model Tuning and Hyperparameter Optimization

Once we have a basic model, the next step is to **optimize** it. This can involve tuning hyperparameters (e.g., the number of trees in a Random Forest, or the learning rate in Gradient Boosting). We can use **GridSearchCV** or **RandomizedSearchCV** in Scikit-learn to find the best combination of hyperparameters.

python

```
from sklearn.model_selection import GridSearchCV

# Define parameter grid for hyperparameter tuning
param_grid = {'n_estimators': [50, 100, 200], 'max_depth': [10, 20, 30]}

# Perform grid search
grid_search         =          GridSearchCV(estimator=RandomForestClassifier(),
param_grid=param_grid, cv=3)
grid_search.fit(X_train, y_train)

# Get the best parameters
print("Best Hyperparameters:", grid_search.best_params_)
```

9.1.8 Step 8: Model Deployment

Once the model is trained, evaluated, and tuned, it can be deployed to make predictions on new data. The deployment process can involve saving the trained model using **joblib** or **pickle**, and then integrating it into a production pipeline for real-time predictions.

python

import joblib

Save the trained model

joblib.dump(model, 'fraud_detection_model.pkl')

9.2 Real-World Case Study: Building a Fraud Detection System

In this section, we'll apply the steps above to build a **fraud detection system** using a public dataset.

9.2.1 Problem Overview

In fraud detection, the goal is to classify transactions as either fraudulent or non-fraudulent. We'll use the **credit card fraud detection dataset** from Kaggle, which contains features such as the transaction amount, time of transaction, and anonymized features (due to privacy concerns).

9.2.2 Loading and Preprocessing the Data

First, we load and preprocess the data, including normalizing numerical features and handling any missing values.

python

```python
import pandas as pd
from sklearn.preprocessing import StandardScaler

# Load the dataset
data = pd.read_csv('creditcard.csv')

# Preprocessing: scaling the numerical features
scaler = StandardScaler()
data['Amount'] = scaler.fit_transform(data['Amount'].values.reshape(-1, 1))

# Split the data into features (X) and target (y)
X = data.drop(columns=['Class'])  # Features
y = data['Class']  # Target variable (0 = non-fraud, 1 = fraud)
```

9.2.3 Model Selection and Training

For fraud detection, we choose a **Random Forest Classifier** due to its ability to handle complex relationships and its robustness to overfitting.

python

```
from sklearn.ensemble import RandomForestClassifier

from sklearn.model_selection import train_test_split


# Split data into training and testing sets

X_train, X_test, y_train, y_test = train_test_split(X, y, test_size=0.2,
random_state=42)


# Initialize and train the model

model = RandomForestClassifier(n_estimators=100, random_state=42)

model.fit(X_train, y_train)
```

9.2.4 Model Evaluation

Next, we evaluate the model using metrics like precision, recall, and F1-score. In fraud detection, it's crucial to have high recall (the ability to identify fraudulent transactions) even at the expense of precision (minimizing false positives).

python

```
from sklearn.metrics import classification_report, confusion_matrix


# Make predictions

y_pred = model.predict(X_test)
```

```
# Evaluate the model
print(classification_report(y_test, y_pred))
```

The output might look like this (example values):

markdown

	precision	recall	f1-score	support
0	1.00	1.00	1.00	284315
1	0.94	0.80	0.86	492
accuracy			1.00	284807
macro avg	0.97	0.90	0.93	284807
weighted avg	1.00	1.00	1.00	284807

From the results, we can see that the model performs well on the majority class (non-fraud), with high accuracy. However, it's also critical to look at recall for the minority class (fraud), as detecting fraudulent transactions is the main objective. Here, we achieve a recall of 0.80, which means 80% of fraudulent transactions are correctly identified.

9.2.5 Model Tuning

Finally, we tune the model using **GridSearchCV** to find the best parameters for the Random Forest Classifier and improve performance.

python

```
from sklearn.model_selection import GridSearchCV

# Parameter grid
param_grid = {'n_estimators': [100, 200, 300], 'max_depth': [10, 20, 30]}

# Grid search
grid_search       =       GridSearchCV(estimator=RandomForestClassifier(),
param_grid=param_grid, cv=3)
grid_search.fit(X_train, y_train)

# Best parameters
print("Best Parameters:", grid_search.best_params_)
```

9.3 Summary of Key Concepts

- **Data Preprocessing**: Cleaning, scaling, and encoding data are essential steps in the workflow.

- **Model Training**: Choosing the right model (e.g., Random Forest) and training it using the .fit() method.

- **Model Evaluation**: Using metrics like accuracy, precision, recall, and F1-score to assess performance, with particular emphasis on recall for imbalanced datasets.

- **Model Tuning**: Optimizing hyperparameters with GridSearchCV to improve model performance.

- **Real-World Application**: We demonstrated these steps using a fraud detection system, where the model identifies fraudulent transactions based on transaction data.

By the end of this chapter, you should have a solid understanding of how to build and evaluate machine learning models with Scikit-learn, along with the practical steps involved in developing a real-world AI application like fraud detection.

CHAPTER 10: DEEP DIVE INTO TENSORFLOW AND KERAS

In this chapter, we'll explore **TensorFlow** and **Keras**, two powerful libraries widely used for building and training neural networks. We'll cover how to set up the environment, build and train a simple neural network, and use it to solve a real-world problem—predicting stock prices. TensorFlow provides the low-level functionalities, while Keras offers a high-level API for quickly building deep learning models, making it ideal for both beginners and experts.

10.1 Setting Up TensorFlow and Keras

Before we dive into building models, let's first ensure that your environment is set up for TensorFlow and Keras.

10.1.1 Installing TensorFlow

To install TensorFlow, you can use **pip**, Python's package installer. Open a terminal and run:

bash

pip install tensorflow

This will install the latest version of TensorFlow, which includes Keras as its high-level API. TensorFlow provides everything you need to build, train, and deploy machine learning models.

10.1.2 Verifying the Installation

Once TensorFlow is installed, you can verify the installation by checking the version:

python

import tensorflow as tf
print(tf._version_)

If everything is set up correctly, this should print the version of TensorFlow you installed.

10.1.3 TensorFlow vs. Keras

- **TensorFlow**: A deep learning framework for building complex neural networks and performing machine learning tasks at scale. It allows fine-grained control over the model and is highly scalable, ideal for large-scale applications.

- **Keras**: Initially developed as a standalone deep learning library, Keras is now a part of TensorFlow. It provides a user-friendly, high-level API for building neural networks quickly and easily.

Although Keras is built on top of TensorFlow, it abstracts many of the complexities of TensorFlow, making it more accessible for fast prototyping.

10.2 Building and Training a Neural Network with Keras

Now, let's dive into building and training a simple neural network using Keras. We will build a basic feedforward neural network (also known as a **fully connected neural network**) to solve a problem of regression.

10.2.1 Data Preparation

For this example, we'll use a dataset to predict stock prices based on historical data. Let's use the **Yahoo Finance API** to fetch historical stock data, which we'll then process for training.

python

```
import yfinance as yf
import pandas as pd

# Fetch historical stock data (e.g., Tesla stock for the past 5 years)
stock_data = yf.download("TSLA", start="2018-01-01", end="2023-01-01")

# Display the first few rows of the dataset
print(stock_data.head())
```

The dataset will include columns like **Open**, **High**, **Low**, **Close**, and **Volume**. We'll use the **Close price** as the target variable for predicting future prices.

10.2.2 Data Preprocessing

We'll need to preprocess the data to prepare it for input into the neural network. This typically involves scaling the data and splitting it into training and testing sets.

- **Feature Scaling**: Neural networks perform better when the input data is scaled, typically using MinMax scaling or Standardization (zero mean, unit variance).

- **Train-Test Split**: We'll split the dataset into training and test sets to evaluate the model's performance on unseen data.

python

```python
from sklearn.preprocessing import MinMaxScaler
from sklearn.model_selection import train_test_split

# Use only the 'Close' price for this example
data = stock_data['Close'].values.reshape(-1, 1)

# Scale the data
scaler = MinMaxScaler(feature_range=(0, 1))
scaled_data = scaler.fit_transform(data)

# Prepare the data for training (use past 60 days' data to predict the next day's price)
X = []
y = []
```

```
for i in range(60, len(scaled_data)):

    X.append(scaled_data[i-60:i, 0])

    y.append(scaled_data[i, 0])


X, y = np.array(X), np.array(y)


# Split the data into training and testing sets (80% train, 20% test)
X_train, X_test, y_train, y_test = train_test_split(X, y, test_size=0.2,
shuffle=False)


# Reshape X_train and X_test for the LSTM network (samples, timesteps,
features)
X_train = X_train.reshape(X_train.shape[0], X_train.shape[1], 1)
X_test = X_test.reshape(X_test.shape[0], X_test.shape[1], 1)
```

10.2.3 Building the Neural Network

For this example, we'll use a **Sequential model** in Keras, which allows us to stack layers in a linear fashion. We'll start with a simple **Dense** (fully connected) layer to predict stock prices. The neural network will have one hidden layer and one output layer.

python

```
from tensorflow.keras.models import Sequential

from tensorflow.keras.layers import Dense, LSTM


# Initialize the Sequential model

model = Sequential()


# Add the LSTM layer (long short-term memory layer) for time-series data

model.add(LSTM(units=50,                          return_sequences=True,

input_shape=(X_train.shape[1], 1)))

model.add(LSTM(units=50, return_sequences=False))


# Add a Dense layer for output

model.add(Dense(units=1))  # Predict the next day's stock price


# Compile the model

model.compile(optimizer='adam', loss='mean_squared_error')


# Summarize the model structure

model.summary()
```

10.2.4 Training the Model

Now that the model is built, we can train it using the training data.

We will use the **mean squared error** loss function, as this is a regression problem, and the **Adam optimizer**, which is commonly used for training deep learning models.

python

```python
# Train the model
model.fit(X_train, y_train, epochs=10, batch_size=32, validation_data=(X_test, y_test))
```

This will train the model for 10 epochs. You can increase the number of epochs for better accuracy if needed.

10.2.5 Evaluating the Model

After training, it's important to evaluate the model's performance on the test set to understand how well it generalizes to unseen data. We can plot the predicted stock prices against the actual stock prices.

python

```python
import matplotlib.pyplot as plt

# Predict stock prices for the test set
y_pred = model.predict(X_test)
```

```
# Invert the scaling to get the actual stock prices

y_pred_actual = scaler.inverse_transform(y_pred)

y_test_actual = scaler.inverse_transform(y_test.reshape(-1, 1))


# Plot the results

plt.plot(y_test_actual, color='blue', label='Actual Stock Price')

plt.plot(y_pred_actual, color='red', label='Predicted Stock Price')

plt.title('Stock Price Prediction')

plt.xlabel('Time')

plt.ylabel('Stock Price')

plt.legend()

plt.show()
```

This will display a graph where the blue line represents the actual stock prices and the red line shows the predicted prices. Ideally, the two lines should be very close to each other, indicating that the model is performing well.

10.3 Real-World Example: Predicting Stock Prices

In this section, we've shown how to use TensorFlow and Keras to build and train a neural network to predict stock prices. This example focused on the **LSTM (Long Short-Term Memory)** network, which is well-suited for time-series forecasting tasks like stock price prediction.

10.3.1 Why Use LSTM for Stock Price Prediction?

LSTM networks are a type of **recurrent neural network (RNN)** that is particularly effective at learning from sequences of data, such as time-series data. Unlike traditional feedforward networks, LSTMs have memory cells that store information across time steps, allowing them to learn long-term dependencies in sequential data—critical for tasks like predicting stock prices.

- **TensorFlow and Keras Setup**: Installing and setting up TensorFlow, which includes Keras as a high-level API for building neural networks.
- **Data Preprocessing**: Scaling and preparing the stock price data for use in the model, including handling time-series data for LSTM networks.

- **Building a Neural Network**: Using Keras to create and train a simple LSTM model for predicting stock prices.

- **Model Evaluation**: Evaluating the model's performance by comparing predicted stock prices with actual prices and visualizing the results.

By the end of this chapter, you should have a strong foundation in how to use TensorFlow and Keras to build deep learning models, particularly for time-series forecasting tasks like stock price prediction.

CHAPTER 11: COMPUTER VISION WITH PYTHON

In this chapter, we'll dive into the exciting field of **Computer Vision**, where machines are able to interpret and understand images and video. We'll explore the basics of image processing, object detection using Python, and build a **facial recognition system** as a case study. Python, with its rich ecosystem of libraries, is a powerful tool for developing and deploying computer vision applications.

11.1 Basics of Image Processing

Before diving into complex tasks like object detection or facial recognition, it's crucial to understand the fundamentals of **image processing**. Images are essentially matrices (arrays) of pixel values. In a grayscale image, each pixel contains a value between 0 and 255, representing the intensity of light, with 0 being black and 255 being white. In color images (such as RGB), each pixel contains three values (Red, Green, Blue), each ranging from 0 to 255.

11.1.1 Loading and Displaying Images with OpenCV

The first step in most computer vision tasks is loading an image. We'll use **OpenCV** (Open Source Computer Vision Library), one of the most popular Python libraries for image processing.

bash

```
pip install opencv-python
```

Here's how to load and display an image using OpenCV:

python

```
import cv2

# Load the image (grayscale mode)
image = cv2.imread('image.jpg', cv2.IMREAD_GRAYSCALE)

# Display the image in a window
cv2.imshow('Grayscale Image', image)

# Wait for a key press and close the window
cv2.waitKey(0)
cv2.destroyAllWindows()
```

This code loads an image, displays it, and waits for the user to press a key to close the window.

11.1.2 Basic Image Operations

Here are some basic image processing operations:

- **Resizing**: Adjusting the dimensions of an image.

  python

  ```
  resized_image = cv2.resize(image, (width, height))
  ```

- **Thresholding**: Converting a grayscale image to a binary image (black and white).

  python

  ```
  _, binary_image = cv2.threshold(image, 127, 255, cv2.THRESH_BINARY)
  ```

- **Edge Detection**: Detecting edges in an image using the **Canny edge detector**.

  python

```
edges = cv2.Canny(image, threshold1=100, threshold2=200)
```

- **Blurring**: Smoothing the image to reduce noise.

python

```
blurred_image = cv2.GaussianBlur(image, (5, 5), 0)
```

These are just a few basic operations. Image processing is a vast field, and understanding these fundamentals helps in more advanced tasks like object detection and facial recognition.

11.2 Object Detection Using Python

Object detection involves identifying and localizing objects in images or videos. It's a key task in computer vision, widely used in applications like surveillance, autonomous vehicles, and facial recognition.

11.2.1 Using Pre-trained Models for Object Detection

A common approach in object detection is using pre-trained models. **Haar Cascades**, a machine learning-based approach, is one such method in OpenCV. It is widely used for detecting faces, eyes, or other objects in real-time.

Here's an example of detecting faces in an image using Haar Cascades:

1. **Load the pre-trained Haar Cascade classifier** (OpenCV provides many pre-trained classifiers for objects like faces, eyes, and cars).

python

```python
# Load pre-trained Haar Cascade classifier for face detection
face_cascade = cv2.CascadeClassifier(cv2.data.haarcascades + 'haarcascade_frontalface_default.xml')

# Load an image
image = cv2.imread('image.jpg')
gray_image = cv2.cvtColor(image, cv2.COLOR_BGR2GRAY)  # Convert to grayscale

# Detect faces in the image
```

```
faces = face_cascade.detectMultiScale(gray_image, scaleFactor=1.1,
minNeighbors=5)


# Draw rectangles around the detected faces
for (x, y, w, h) in faces:
    cv2.rectangle(image, (x, y), (x + w, y + h), (0, 255, 0), 2)


# Display the image with detected faces
cv2.imshow('Faces Detected', image)
cv2.waitKey(0)
cv2.destroyAllWindows()
```

This code loads a pre-trained **Haar Cascade** classifier and uses it to detect faces in an image. The detectMultiScale() function returns the coordinates of any faces detected in the image.

11.2.2 Advanced Object Detection with Deep Learning Models

While Haar Cascades are fast, they are not as accurate as modern deep learning models. For more complex object detection tasks, we can use pre-trained **Convolutional Neural Networks (CNNs)** and models such as **YOLO (You Only Look Once)** or **SSD (Single Shot Multibox Detector)**.

For object detection using deep learning, you can use **TensorFlow** and its **Object Detection API**. It provides a wide range of pre-trained models that can be fine-tuned for specific tasks.

11.3 Case Study: Building a Facial Recognition System

Facial recognition is one of the most popular applications of computer vision. The idea is to identify and verify individuals based on their facial features.

11.3.1 Face Detection and Recognition Workflow

Facial recognition typically involves two steps:

1. **Face Detection**: Identifying and locating faces in images or video frames.

2. **Face Recognition**: Identifying the person based on the detected face by comparing it to a database of known faces.

We'll use **OpenCV** for face detection and **Face Recognition** library for face recognition.

11.3.2 Install the Required Libraries

bash

pip install opencv-python face-recognition

- **OpenCV** will be used for face detection.

- **Face Recognition** is a powerful library built on top of **dlib** that makes face recognition tasks much easier.

11.3.3 Face Detection with OpenCV

We'll first detect the face(s) in an image using the Haar Cascade classifier, similar to what we did in the object detection section.

python

```
import cv2

# Load the pre-trained Haar Cascade classifier for face detection
face_cascade = cv2.CascadeClassifier(cv2.data.haarcascades + 'haarcascade_frontalface_default.xml')

# Load the image
image = cv2.imread('image.jpg')
```

```
gray_image = cv2.cvtColor(image, cv2.COLOR_BGR2GRAY)


# Detect faces

faces    =    face_cascade.detectMultiScale(gray_image,    scaleFactor=1.1,

minNeighbors=5)


# Draw rectangles around detected faces

for (x, y, w, h) in faces:

    cv2.rectangle(image, (x, y), (x + w, y + h), (0, 255, 0), 2)


# Show the image with faces detected

cv2.imshow('Faces Detected', image)

cv2.waitKey(0)

cv2.destroyAllWindows()
```

11.3.4 Face Recognition

After detecting faces, we can use the **Face Recognition** library to identify individuals. Here's how to load an image, detect faces, and compare them to a database of known faces.

1. **Load and Encode Faces**: First, we need to load images of known people and encode their faces.

python

```python
import face_recognition

# Load a sample image of a known person
known_image = face_recognition.load_image_file("known_person.jpg")
known_encoding = face_recognition.face_encodings(known_image)[0]

# Store the known face encoding in a list (for simplicity, we'll only store one face)
known_faces = [known_encoding]
known_names = ["Person Name"]
```

2. **Detect and Recognize Faces in a New Image**:

python

```python
# Load an image with an unknown person
unknown_image = face_recognition.load_image_file("unknown_person.jpg")

# Find all face locations and face encodings in the image
unknown_face_locations = face_recognition.face_locations(unknown_image)
unknown_face_encodings = face_recognition.face_encodings(unknown_image,
unknown_face_locations)
```

```python
# Compare the unknown faces with the known faces
for unknown_encoding, unknown_location in zip(unknown_face_encodings,
unknown_face_locations):
    matches = face_recognition.compare_faces(known_faces,
unknown_encoding)

    name = "Unknown"
    if True in matches:
        first_match_index = matches.index(True)
        name = known_names[first_match_index]

    # Draw a rectangle around the face and label it with the name
    top, right, bottom, left = unknown_location
    cv2.rectangle(unknown_image, (left, top), (right, bottom), (0, 255, 0), 2)
    cv2.putText(unknown_image, name, (left + 6, bottom - 6),
cv2.FONT_HERSHEY_DUPLEX, 0.5, (0, 0, 255), 1)

# Display the result
cv2.imshow('Face Recognition Result', unknown_image)
cv2.waitKey(0)
cv2.destroyAllWindows()
```

This code first encodes the known faces and then compares them to faces detected in a new image. If a match is found, the system labels the face with the corresponding name.

- **Image Processing Basics**: Loading, displaying, resizing, thresholding, edge detection, and blurring images using OpenCV.

- **Object Detection**: Using Haar Cascades for simple object detection and deep learning models (YOLO, SSD) for more complex detection tasks.

- **Facial Recognition**: Using OpenCV and the **Face Recognition** library to detect and recognize faces in images.

By the end of this chapter, you should be able to build a simple facial recognition system and understand the fundamentals of object detection and image processing in Python. You will also have experience using libraries like OpenCV and Face Recognition to implement real-world computer vision applications.

CHAPTER 12: REINFORCEMENT LEARNING BASICS

In this chapter, we will introduce **Reinforcement Learning (RL)**, a type of machine learning where an agent learns to make decisions by interacting with its environment. The key to RL is that the agent takes actions, receives feedback (rewards or punishments), and learns to optimize its decisions to achieve long-term goals. RL is widely used in applications like robotics, game playing, autonomous vehicles, and optimization problems.

We'll cover the core concepts of reinforcement learning, including **Markov Decision Processes (MDPs)** and **Q-learning**, and end with a simple example of building an agent that learns to play a basic game.

12.1 Introduction to Reinforcement Learning Concepts

Reinforcement learning is different from supervised and unsupervised learning because, in RL, the agent does not have access to labeled data. Instead, the agent interacts with an environment and learns by trial and error, improving its performance over time based on feedback (rewards).

Key concepts in reinforcement learning include:

- **Agent**: The entity that makes decisions and learns to take actions in an environment.

- **Environment**: Everything the agent interacts with and makes decisions about.

- **State (s)**: A representation of the environment at a given time. States contain all the information needed for the agent to make decisions.

- **Action (a)**: A decision or move made by the agent that changes the state of the environment.

- **Reward (r)**: A numerical value the agent receives after performing an action. The reward indicates the immediate benefit or cost of an action.

- **Policy (π)**: A strategy or rule that maps states to actions. The policy dictates how the agent behaves in different situations.

- **Value Function (V)**: A function that estimates the long-term reward expected from a state, guiding the agent's decision-making.

- **Q-function (Q)**: A function that estimates the expected reward from taking a specific action in a specific state.

The goal of an RL agent is to learn the optimal policy that maximizes the cumulative reward over time.

12.2 Markov Decision Processes (MDPs)

The foundation of reinforcement learning is the **Markov Decision Process (MDP)**. An MDP is a mathematical model for decision-making, where an agent interacts with an environment in discrete time steps. It consists of:

- **States (S)**: The set of all possible states the agent can be in.

- **Actions (A)**: The set of all possible actions the agent can take.

- **Transition Function (T)**: Describes the probability of transitioning from one state to another after taking an action.

P(s'|s,a)=P(next state s'|current state s,action a)P(s'|s, a) = P(\text{next state } s' | \text{current state } s, \text{action } a)P(s'|s,a)=P(next state s'|current state s,action a)

- **Reward Function (R)**: A function that provides feedback to the agent based on the state-action pair, indicating the immediate benefit or cost.

R(s,a)→rewardR(s, a) \rightarrow \text{reward}R(s,a)→reward

- **Discount Factor (γ)**: A value between 0 and 1 that discounts the future rewards. The discount factor balances immediate rewards versus long-term rewards.

The agent's goal is to choose actions that maximize the total discounted reward over time. The total return (or reward) the agent aims to maximize is represented as:

Gt=Rt+γRt+1+γ2Rt+2+...G_t = R_t + \gamma R_{t+1} + \gamma^2 R_{t+2} + \dotsGt=Rt+γRt+1+γ2Rt+2+...

Where:

- GtG_tGt is the total return starting at time step ttt.

- RtR_tRt is the immediate reward received at time step ttt.

- γ\gammaγ is the discount factor.

An important aspect of MDPs is that they follow the **Markov property**, which means the future state depends only on the current state and action, not on the sequence of states that preceded it. This property allows RL problems to be modeled efficiently.

12.3 Q-learning: A Model-Free Reinforcement Learning Algorithm

Q-learning is one of the most popular algorithms used in reinforcement learning. It is a **model-free** algorithm, meaning the agent does not need to know the transition function $P(s'|s,a)P(s'|s,a)P(s'|s,a)$ or the reward function $R(s,a)R(s, a)R(s,a)$ beforehand.

Instead, the agent learns the optimal policy directly from interactions with the environment by updating the **Q-values**.

The **Q-value** (also called the **action-value**) represents the expected return (reward) of taking an action aaa in a state sss, and following the best policy thereafter:

$Q(s,a)=E[rt+\gamma \cdot max$⌊fo⌋$a'Q(s',a')|s0=s,a0=a]Q(s, a) = \mathbb{E}[r\_t + \gamma \cdot \max\_{a'} Q(s', a') | s\_0 = s, a\_0 = a]Q(s,a)=E[rt +\gamma \cdot a'maxQ(s',a')|s0=s,a0=a]$

Where:

- $Q(s,a)Q(s, a)Q(s,a)$ is the Q-value for state sss and action aaa.
- rtr_trt is the reward at time ttt.
- $\gamma \gamma\gamma$ is the discount factor.
- max⌊fo⌋$a'Q(s',a')\max\_{a'} Q(s', a')maxa'Q(s',a')$ is the maximum Q-value for the next state s's's'.

The Q-learning algorithm updates the Q-values iteratively based on the following **Bellman equation**:

$Q(s,a)\leftarrow Q(s,a)+\alpha\cdot[r+\gamma\cdot\max_{a'}Q(s',a')-Q(s,a)]Q(s, a) \leftarrow Q(s, a) + \alpha \cdot \left[r + \gamma \cdot \max_{a'} Q(s', a') - Q(s, a) \right]Q(s,a)\leftarrow Q(s,a)+\alpha\cdot[r+\gamma\cdot a'\max Q(s',a')-Q(s,a)]$

Where:

- α\alpha$\alpha$ is the **learning rate**, which controls how quickly the algorithm updates the Q-values.

- rrr is the immediate reward.

- γ\gamma$\gamma$ is the discount factor.

- $\max_{a'}Q(s',a')$\max_{a'} Q(s', a')$\max_{a'}Q(s',a')$ is the maximum Q-value for the next state.

The algorithm works by:

1. Initializing the Q-values for all state-action pairs (often to 0).

2. Observing the current state.

3. Taking an action based on an exploration-exploitation strategy (e.g., **epsilon-greedy**).

4. Receiving the reward and transitioning to a new state.

5. Updating the Q-values using the Bellman equation.

6. Repeating the process until convergence (i.e., the Q-values stop changing).

12.4 Simple Example: Building a Game Agent with Q-learning

Let's apply Q-learning to a simple game environment. Consider a basic **grid-world** game where an agent moves around a grid. The agent receives a reward based on its position and must learn the optimal actions to reach a goal.

12.4.1 Grid-World Environment

Here's a simple 4x4 grid environment where:

- The agent starts at the top-left corner (0,0).

- The goal is at the bottom-right corner (3,3).

- The agent can move **up, down, left**, or **right**.

- The agent receives a reward of +1 when it reaches the goal and -1 for every step taken.

12.4.2 Q-learning Implementation

Let's implement the Q-learning algorithm to train the agent.

```python
python

import numpy as np
import random

# Define the environment
grid_size = 4
goal_state = (3, 3)
start_state = (0, 0)

# Initialize the Q-table (state-action values)
Q = np.zeros((grid_size, grid_size, 4))  # 4 possible actions: up, down, left, right

# Define the actions (0: up, 1: down, 2: left, 3: right)
actions = [(-1, 0), (1, 0), (0, -1), (0, 1)]  # (delta_x, delta_y)

# Parameters
learning_rate = 0.1
discount_factor = 0.9
epsilon = 0.1  # Exploration rate
episodes = 1000

def take_action(state, action):
```

```
    """Move the agent based on the action taken."""
    x, y = state
    dx, dy = actions[action]
    x_new, y_new = x + dx, y + dy

    # Ensure the agent stays within the grid
    x_new = max(0, min(x_new, grid_size - 1))
    y_new = max(0, min(y_new, grid_size - 1))

    return (x_new, y_new)


def get_reward(state):
    """Return the reward for a given state."""
    if state == goal_state:
        return 1  # Reward for reaching the goal
    return -0.1  # Small penalty for each move


def epsilon_greedy(state):
    """Choose an action using epsilon-greedy policy."""
    if random.uniform(0, 1) < epsilon:
        # Explore: choose a random action
        return random.randint(0, 3)
    else:
```

```python
        # Exploit: choose the best action based on Q-values
        return np.argmax(Q[state[0], state[1]])


# Train the agent
for episode in range(episodes):
    state = start_state
    while state != goal_state:
        action = epsilon_greedy(state)
        next_state = take_action(state, action)
        reward = get_reward(next_state)


        # Update the Q-value
        next_max = np.max(Q[next_state[0], next_state[1]])  # Max Q-value for the
next state
        Q[state[0], state[1], action] = Q[state[0], state[1], action] + learning_rate *
(reward + discount_factor * next_max - Q[state[0], state[1], action])


        # Move to the next state
        state = next_state


print("Training complete!")
```

12.4.3 Explanation

In this code:

- We define a **4x4 grid** environment where the agent's goal is to move from the start state $(0, 0)$ to the goal state $(3, 3)$.

- The agent learns to take actions (up, down, left, right) by interacting with the environment.

- The **Q-table** is used to store the Q-values for each state-action pair.

- The agent uses the **epsilon-greedy policy** to balance exploration (random actions) and exploitation (choosing the best-known action based on the current Q-values).

- Over many episodes, the Q-values converge to reflect the optimal policy for navigating the grid.

- **Reinforcement Learning**: The agent learns through trial and error, interacting with the environment, and receiving rewards for actions.

- **MDP**: A framework for modeling decision-making problems, consisting of states, actions, rewards, and transitions.

- **Q-learning**: A model-free algorithm that learns the optimal policy by updating Q-values iteratively.

- **Game Agent Example**: We used Q-learning to train a simple agent to navigate a grid-world environment and reach a goal.

CHAPTER 13: BUILDING INTELLIGENT SYSTEMS WITH PYTHON

In this chapter, we'll explore how to leverage **AI models** to build **intelligent systems** for real-world applications across various industries such as **finance, healthcare**, and more. You'll learn how to integrate AI models into larger systems, where these models can make decisions, automate processes, and provide insights. The goal is to show you how Python, with its rich ecosystem of libraries, can be used to develop end-to-end solutions that deliver impactful results in real-world scenarios.

13.1 AI in Real-World Applications

AI has already made a significant impact across various industries, enabling smarter, faster, and more efficient systems. Let's look at some key sectors where AI is being applied.

13.1.1 AI in Finance

In the financial industry, AI is used for tasks like fraud detection, algorithmic trading, and risk assessment. AI models can analyze large volumes of data to spot patterns, predict market trends, and help financial institutions make data-driven decisions.

- **Fraud Detection**: Machine learning models can detect fraudulent transactions by identifying patterns that deviate from normal behavior. This is typically done using supervised learning algorithms (e.g., logistic regression, random forests, neural networks) trained on historical transaction data.

- **Algorithmic Trading**: AI-powered trading algorithms use techniques such as reinforcement learning and deep learning to make buy/sell decisions. These algorithms continuously learn from market conditions and improve their decision-making over time.

- **Credit Scoring and Risk Assessment**: AI models help lenders evaluate the risk of lending to a borrower by analyzing their financial history, behavior patterns, and other relevant data.

13.1.2 AI in Healthcare

AI has the potential to revolutionize healthcare by improving diagnosis, treatment planning, and patient care. Some applications include:

- **Medical Imaging and Diagnostics**: Convolutional Neural Networks (CNNs) are used to analyze medical images (e.g., X-rays, MRIs) and assist doctors in diagnosing diseases like cancer, heart conditions, and more. These models can detect subtle patterns that are difficult for human eyes to see.

- **Predictive Analytics**: AI models can predict patient outcomes (e.g., likelihood of readmission, risk of complications) by analyzing historical patient data. These models help healthcare providers make proactive decisions and optimize resource allocation.

- **Personalized Medicine**: AI can recommend personalized treatment plans based on an individual's genetic makeup, medical history, and current health conditions. This allows for more precise and effective treatment.

13.1.3 AI in Other Industries

- **Retail**: AI is used for recommendation systems, customer segmentation, and inventory management. For instance, e-commerce platforms like Amazon use AI to recommend products based on past behavior and preferences.

- **Transportation**: Autonomous vehicles, route optimization for delivery services, and predictive maintenance for machinery are some applications of AI in transportation.

- **Energy**: AI helps optimize energy consumption, predict equipment failures, and enhance the efficiency of energy grids by analyzing real-time data from sensors.

13.2 Integrating AI Models into Larger Applications

Building intelligent systems isn't just about creating a powerful model; it's about integrating that model into a larger system that interacts with other services, APIs, databases, and user interfaces. In this section, we'll walk through the key steps involved in integrating AI models into production systems.

13.2.1 Designing an AI-Enabled Application

When building an intelligent application, it's essential to consider the following components:

- **Data Pipeline**: The first step is to collect, clean, and preprocess data from various sources (e.g., databases, APIs, IoT devices). This data will be used to train and test your AI models.

- **Model Development**: Develop the machine learning or deep learning models suited to your application. This may involve tasks like feature engineering, model selection, training, and validation. Python libraries like **Scikit-learn**, **TensorFlow**, and **PyTorch** are commonly used for this purpose.

- **Model Deployment**: Once your model is trained, it needs to be deployed into a production environment where it can start making predictions or decisions in real-time. This may involve using cloud platforms (e.g., AWS, Google Cloud, Azure), Docker containers, or other deployment frameworks.

- **APIs for Interaction**: Create APIs that allow other systems or users to interact with your AI model. These APIs can handle requests like making predictions, processing data, or performing specific tasks based on user input.

- **User Interface (UI)**: For end-users to interact with your system, you'll need a front-end interface (web or mobile) where users can input data and see results. This may involve creating a **dashboard** for data visualization or reporting.

13.2.2 Model Deployment Tools and Frameworks

Several tools and frameworks can help deploy AI models into production systems:

- **Flask / FastAPI**: These lightweight web frameworks allow you to create REST APIs for your AI models. You can easily expose model predictions as endpoints that can be accessed by other applications.

Example (using Flask to deploy a simple ML model):

python

```python
from flask import Flask, request, jsonify
import joblib

app = Flask(__name__)

# Load a pre-trained model
model = joblib.load('model.pkl')

@app.route('/predict', methods=['POST'])
def predict():
    data = request.get_json()  # Get input data
    prediction = model.predict([data['input']])  # Make prediction
    return jsonify({'prediction': prediction.tolist()})

if __name__ == '__main__':
    app.run(debug=True)
```

- **TensorFlow Serving**: A flexible, high-performance serving system for deploying machine learning models. It supports

TensorFlow models and other types (e.g., PyTorch models), and it's designed for production environments.

- **Docker**: Docker allows you to package your AI model and all its dependencies into a container, ensuring that it runs consistently across different environments. Docker containers can be deployed on cloud platforms or on-premises.

- **Kubernetes**: For large-scale deployment, Kubernetes is an open-source system for automating the deployment, scaling, and management of containerized applications. You can use Kubernetes to deploy AI models in a distributed setting.

13.2.3 Monitoring and Maintenance of AI Models

Once the AI model is deployed, it's important to monitor its performance and ensure it continues to deliver accurate results. Over time, models can become outdated due to changes in the underlying data distribution (a phenomenon known as **model drift**). To manage this, you can implement:

- **Continuous Monitoring**: Track model performance in real-time to ensure it's making accurate predictions. If the model's performance drops below a certain threshold, it may need retraining.

- **Model Retraining**: Based on feedback from the deployed system or new data, the model may need to be retrained periodically to adapt to changes in the environment.

- **Version Control**: Maintain versions of the model and its training data to easily roll back to a previous version if needed. Tools like **MLflow** and **DVC** (Data Version Control) are helpful for managing machine learning experiments and models.

13.3 Case Study: Building a Credit Scoring System for Finance

Let's go through an example of how AI can be applied in finance by building a **credit scoring system**. This system will predict whether a loan applicant is likely to default on a loan based on their financial data.

13.3.1 Data Collection and Preprocessing

We'll collect data on applicants, including features like:

- Credit history

- Income level

- Loan amount

- Employment status

We clean the data by handling missing values, encoding categorical variables, and normalizing numerical values.

13.3.2 Model Development

We choose a classification algorithm, such as **logistic regression** or **random forest**, and train it on historical data of applicants and their loan repayment history.

python

```
from sklearn.ensemble import RandomForestClassifier
from sklearn.model_selection import train_test_split
from sklearn.metrics import accuracy_score
```

```
# Assuming data is a pandas DataFrame

X = data.drop('default', axis=1)  # Features

y = data['default']  # Target (1 = default, 0 = no default)


X_train, X_test, y_train, y_test = train_test_split(X, y, test_size=0.2)


model = RandomForestClassifier()

model.fit(X_train, y_train)


# Predictions

y_pred = model.predict(X_test)


# Evaluate

accuracy = accuracy_score(y_test, y_pred)

print(f"Accuracy: {accuracy}")
```

13.3.3 Model Deployment and Integration

We then deploy the trained model as a REST API using **Flask** or **FastAPI**, where financial institutions can input new applicant data and get a prediction on whether they are likely to default on the loan.

- **AI in Real-World Applications**: We've covered several industries where AI is making an impact, including finance, healthcare, and retail.

- **Integrating AI into Larger Systems**: We discussed how to design, deploy, and maintain intelligent systems, using APIs, cloud platforms, and monitoring tools.

- **Case Study**: We went through the process of building and deploying a credit scoring system for the finance industry.

By the end of this chapter, you should have a solid understanding of how to build AI-powered applications, deploy them into production, and monitor their performance over time.

CHAPTER 14: MODEL EVALUATION AND OPTIMIZATION

In this chapter, we will focus on **evaluating the performance** of machine learning models and exploring techniques for **optimizing** them to ensure they provide the best results. Evaluation is critical because the performance of a model isn't just about how well it fits the training data—it's about how well it generalizes to unseen data. **Model optimization** further enhances this generalization by fine-tuning the model to minimize errors and maximize its predictive power.

We'll dive into essential **evaluation metrics**, cover how to **tune hyperparameters**, and introduce **cross-validation**. Finally, we'll walk through a real-world example of improving model performance.

14.1 Metrics for Model Evaluation

To evaluate a model's performance, we rely on various **metrics** that measure how well the model predicts the outcomes. The choice of metric depends on the specific problem (classification, regression, etc.) and what aspect of performance is most important.

14.1.1 Classification Metrics

In classification tasks (e.g., predicting whether an email is spam or not), common evaluation metrics include:

- **Accuracy**: The ratio of correctly predicted instances to the total instances in the dataset. It is a general metric but can be misleading in cases of imbalanced datasets.

  Accuracy=Correct PredictionsTotal Predictions\text{Accuracy} = \frac{\text{Correct Predictions}}{\text{Total Predictions}}Accuracy=Total PredictionsCorrect Predictions

- **Precision**: Precision is the ratio of true positives (correct positive predictions) to all positive predictions (both true positives and false positives). It is important when the cost of false positives is high (e.g., spam detection).

Precision=True PositivesTrue Positives + False Positives\text{Precision} = \frac{\text{True Positives}}{\text{True Positives + False Positives}}Precision=True Positives + False PositivesTrue Positives

- **Recall (Sensitivity)**: Recall is the ratio of true positives to all actual positive instances (true positives and false negatives). Recall is important when the cost of false negatives is high (e.g., medical diagnoses).

Recall=True PositivesTrue Positives + False Negatives\text{Recall} = \frac{\text{True Positives}}{\text{True Positives + False Negatives}}Recall=True Positives + False NegativesTrue Positives

- **F1-Score**: The F1-score is the harmonic mean of precision and recall. It balances the two metrics and is useful when you need a single measure of model performance. A high F1-score indicates both high precision and recall.

F1-Score=2·Precision·RecallPrecision + Recall\text{F1-Score} = 2 \cdot \frac{\text{Precision} \cdot \text{Recall}}{\text{Precision} + Recall}}F1-Score=2·Precision + RecallPrecision·Recall

These metrics provide a deeper understanding of model performance, especially in cases of imbalanced datasets where accuracy alone might not be a good indicator.

14.1.2 Regression Metrics

For regression tasks (e.g., predicting house prices), common evaluation metrics include:

- **Mean Absolute Error (MAE)**: The average of the absolute differences between predicted and actual values.

MAE=1n∑i=1n|yi−y^i|\text{MAE} = \frac{1}{n} \sum_{i=1}^{n} |y_i - \hat{y}_i|MAE=n1i=1∑n|yi−y^i|

- **Mean Squared Error (MSE)**: The average of the squared differences between predicted and actual values. MSE penalizes large errors more than MAE.

MSE=1n∑i=1n(yi−y^i)2\text{MSE} = \frac{1}{n} \sum_{i=1}^{n} (y_i - \hat{y}_i)^2MSE=n1i=1∑n(yi−y^i)2

- **Root Mean Squared Error (RMSE)**: The square root of MSE. RMSE gives a better sense of the magnitude of error in the original scale of the data.

RMSE=MSE\text{RMSE} = \sqrt{\text{MSE}}RMSE=MSE

- **R-squared (R^2)**: A measure of how well the model explains the variance in the target variable. An R^2 value close to 1 indicates a model that fits the data well, while a value close to 0 suggests a poor fit.

$$R2=1-\sum i=1n(yi-y^i)2\sum i=1n(yi-y^-)2R^2 \quad = \quad 1 \quad -$$

\frac{\sum_{i=1}^{n} (y_i - \hat{y}_i)^2}{\sum_{i=1}^{n} (y_i - \bar{y})^2}R2=1-\sum i=1n(yi-y^-)2\sum i=1n(yi-y^i)2

14.2 Hyperparameter Tuning and Cross-Validation

14.2.1 Hyperparameter Tuning

In machine learning, **hyperparameters** are parameters that are not learned from the data, but set before the learning process begins. Examples include:

- **Learning rate** in gradient descent algorithms.
- **Max depth** in decision trees.
- **Number of layers** in a neural network.
- **C** in support vector machines (SVM).

Tuning these hyperparameters is crucial because they directly affect the performance of the model. The process of hyperparameter tuning involves finding the best combination of hyperparameters that leads to the highest model performance.

Common techniques for hyperparameter tuning include:

- **Grid Search**: A brute-force method that tries every combination of hyperparameters in a specified grid. While exhaustive, it can be computationally expensive.

python

```
from sklearn.model_selection import GridSearchCV
param_grid = {
    'max_depth': [3, 5, 7],
    'n_estimators': [100, 200, 300],
}
grid_search          =          GridSearchCV(estimator=model,
param_grid=param_grid, cv=3)
grid_search.fit(X_train, y_train)
best_params = grid_search.best_params_
```

- **Random Search**: Randomly selects combinations of hyperparameters, which is faster than grid search but may not always find the optimal combination.

python

```
from sklearn.model_selection import RandomizedSearchCV
param_dist = {
    'max_depth': [3, 5, 7, 10],
    'n_estimators': [100, 150, 200, 250],
}
random_search         =         RandomizedSearchCV(estimator=model,
param_distributions=param_dist, n_iter=10, cv=3)
random_search.fit(X_train, y_train)
best_params = random_search.best_params_
```

- **Bayesian Optimization**: A more advanced method that uses probability to model the performance of different hyperparameter combinations and searches the space in a more efficient way.

14.2.2 Cross-Validation

Cross-validation is a technique for assessing how well a model generalizes to new, unseen data. It helps reduce the likelihood of overfitting. The most common type of cross-validation is **k-fold cross-validation**:

1. Split the dataset into kkk equally-sized folds (subsets).

2. Train the model on k−1k-1k−1 folds and test it on the remaining fold.

3. Repeat the process kkk times, each time using a different fold as the test set.

4. Average the performance metrics from all kkk tests.

python

```
from sklearn.model_selection import cross_val_score
model = RandomForestClassifier()
scores = cross_val_score(model, X, y, cv=5)  # 5-fold cross-validation
print(f'Cross-validation scores: {scores}')
```

Cross-validation provides a more reliable estimate of model performance than using a single train-test split. It is especially useful when dealing with small datasets.

14.3 Real-World Example: Improving Model Performance

Let's consider a real-world example of **improving model performance** for a **classification task**. Suppose you're building a model to predict whether a customer will churn (leave) a service based on various features like age, contract type, and service usage.

Step 1: Initial Model Evaluation

You start by training a random forest classifier and evaluating it using accuracy.

python

```
from sklearn.ensemble import RandomForestClassifier
from sklearn.metrics import accuracy_score

# Train the model
model = RandomForestClassifier(n_estimators=100)
model.fit(X_train, y_train)

# Predictions
y_pred = model.predict(X_test)
```

```
# Evaluate using accuracy
accuracy = accuracy_score(y_test, y_pred)
print(f'Accuracy: {accuracy}')
```

The model performs reasonably well, but you notice that accuracy isn't the best metric because the dataset is imbalanced (more customers who stay than those who churn).

Step 2: Re-Evaluation with Precision, Recall, and F1-Score

You decide to use **precision**, **recall**, and **F1-score** to get a more balanced view of performance. These metrics will help you assess how well the model identifies the minority class (customers who churn).

python

```
from sklearn.metrics import precision_score, recall_score, f1_score


# Evaluate precision, recall, and F1-score
precision = precision_score(y_test, y_pred)
recall = recall_score(y_test, y_pred)
f1 = f1_score(y_test, y_pred)
```

```
print(f'Precision: {precision}')
```

```
print(f'Recall: {recall}')
```

```
print(f'F1-Score: {f1}')
```

After evaluating these metrics, you see that while recall is high, precision is low, meaning the model is predicting too many customers as likely to churn (false positives).

Step 3: Hyperparameter Tuning

To improve precision, you decide to tune the hyperparameters of the random forest classifier. You use **grid search** to find the best combination of max_depth and n_estimators.

python

```python
from sklearn.model_selection import GridSearchCV

param_grid = {
    'max_depth': [3, 5, 7],
    'n_estimators': [100, 200, 300],
}
```

```
grid_search        =        GridSearchCV(estimator=RandomForestClassifier(),
param_grid=param_grid, cv=3)
grid_search.fit(X_train, y_train)


best_params = grid_search.best_params_
print(f'Best hyperparameters: {best_params}')
```

Step 4: Cross-Validation

Finally, to ensure that the improvements generalize well, you perform **k-fold cross-validation**. This helps you verify that your model performs consistently across different subsets of the data.

python

```
from sklearn.model_selection import cross_val_score


# 5-fold cross-validation
scores = cross_val_score(grid_search.best_estimator_, X, y, cv=5)
print(f'Cross-validation scores: {scores}')
print(f'Mean cross-validation score: {scores.mean()}')
```

By combining **hyperparameter tuning**, **cross-validation**, and careful evaluation using relevant metrics, you successfully improve the model's performance.

- **Evaluation Metrics**: Different metrics such as accuracy, precision, recall, and F1-score help assess the performance of classification models. For regression, metrics like MAE, MSE, and R^2 are commonly used.

- **Hyperparameter Tuning**: Techniques like grid search and random search help optimize the performance of machine learning models by fine-tuning hyperparameters.

- **Cross-Validation**: A method to ensure that a model generalizes well to unseen data by splitting the data into multiple folds for training and testing.

- **Improving Model Performance**: The example demonstrates how tuning hyperparameters and using appropriate evaluation metrics can significantly enhance the performance of a machine learning model.

By the end of this chapter, you should have a solid understanding of how to evaluate machine learning models, fine-tune their hyperparameters, and use cross-validation to ensure robust performance.

CHAPTER 15: WORKING WITH BIG DATA

In this chapter, we will explore how to handle large-scale datasets—what we refer to as **Big Data**—when working with AI and machine learning models. We'll discuss the importance of Big Data frameworks like **Apache Spark** and **Hadoop**, and introduce the techniques used to handle, process, and analyze vast amounts of data that are typically too large to fit in memory. The chapter will culminate with a real-world case study demonstrating how AI models can be used for **real-time data analytics**.

15.1 Introduction to Big Data Frameworks

Big Data refers to datasets that are so large and complex that traditional data processing tools cannot handle them effectively. With the rise of the **Internet of Things (IoT), social media**, and various other data-generating technologies, the amount of data generated each day is growing exponentially. AI and machine learning require robust systems and frameworks to process and analyze this data efficiently.

Two of the most widely used frameworks for Big Data processing are **Apache Spark** and **Hadoop**.

15.1.1 Apache Spark

Apache Spark is an open-source, distributed computing system that can handle large-scale data processing. It is designed to be faster and more general-purpose than its predecessor, Hadoop's MapReduce. Spark can process data in **batch** and **real-time** and supports various programming languages, including **Python**, **Java**, **Scala**, and **R**.

Key features of Spark:

- **In-memory processing**: Spark performs computations in memory (RAM), which makes it significantly faster than Hadoop's MapReduce, which writes intermediate data to disk.

- **Ease of use**: Spark provides high-level APIs for working with data in a more user-friendly way. It also includes libraries for **machine learning** (MLlib), **streaming data** (Spark Streaming), and **graph processing** (GraphX).

- **Scalability**: Spark can scale to handle massive datasets, processing data across multiple machines in a distributed cluster.

15.1.2 Hadoop

Hadoop is another open-source framework designed for processing and storing large datasets in a distributed environment. It uses a **distributed file system (HDFS)** and **MapReduce** for parallel data processing.

Key features of Hadoop:

- **Distributed Storage**: Hadoop's HDFS splits large datasets into blocks and distributes them across a cluster of machines, ensuring data is stored in a fault-tolerant and scalable manner.

- **MapReduce**: The Hadoop processing model involves dividing tasks into smaller units (mappers) and processing them in parallel (reducers). This is ideal for batch processing large datasets.

- **Flexibility**: Hadoop can work with a wide variety of data sources and formats, including structured, semi-structured, and unstructured data.

While Spark is generally preferred for real-time data processing and advanced analytics, Hadoop remains widely used for batch processing and storing large amounts of data over time.

15.2 Data Handling Techniques for AI Models

When working with Big Data, AI models face unique challenges, such as data preprocessing, distributed computing, and model training at scale. Let's look at some of the key techniques used to handle data effectively for machine learning and AI models.

15.2.1 Data Preprocessing for Big Data

Working with Big Data requires more advanced preprocessing techniques to clean, transform, and structure the data. Common preprocessing steps include:

- **Data Sampling**: When dealing with vast amounts of data, it's often impractical to use all the data. Sampling techniques (e.g., random sampling, stratified sampling) can be used to create smaller representative datasets for model training without compromising the integrity of the results.

- **Data Partitioning**: Big Data is typically split into partitions that can be processed independently across multiple machines in a distributed system. Partitioning ensures that data is distributed evenly across the nodes in a cluster for efficient processing.

- **Feature Engineering**: With large datasets, it's often necessary to perform automated feature extraction techniques to generate the most relevant features for the AI models. In Big Data systems, **feature extraction** and **dimensionality reduction** techniques like **Principal**

Component Analysis (PCA) or t-SNE can be used to reduce the dataset size while preserving essential information.

- **Data Normalization/Standardization**: For machine learning models to work effectively, especially with high-dimensional data, normalizing or standardizing data is crucial. Spark and Hadoop allow data transformations across distributed systems to ensure consistent data scaling.

15.2.2 Distributed Computing for Training AI Models

Training machine learning models on large datasets often requires distributed computing. Here's how Big Data frameworks can facilitate the training process:

- **Distributed Data Processing**: Both Spark and Hadoop allow data to be processed in parallel across multiple machines, significantly speeding up the training process. This is particularly important when training **deep learning models** that require massive computational power.

- **Distributed Machine Learning Libraries**: In Spark, the **MLlib** library provides tools for scalable machine learning. MLlib supports distributed versions of common algorithms like regression, classification, and clustering, enabling large datasets to be processed efficiently.

Example: Using Spark's MLlib for distributed logistic regression

python

```
from pyspark.ml.classification import LogisticRegression
from pyspark.ml.feature import VectorAssembler

# Load data
data = spark.read.csv('big_data.csv', header=True, inferSchema=True)

# Feature engineering
assembler = VectorAssembler(inputCols=['feature1', 'feature2', 'feature3'], outputCol='features')
assembled_data = assembler.transform(data)
```

```
# Train model

lr = LogisticRegression(featuresCol='features', labelCol='label')

lr_model = lr.fit(assembled_data)


# Make predictions

predictions = lr_model.transform(assembled_data)
```

- **Scaling Up with Cloud Computing**: Big Data frameworks like Spark and Hadoop are often run on cloud services like **AWS**, **Google Cloud**, or **Microsoft Azure**, which offer scalable compute resources. These platforms allow you to scale your machine learning models to handle petabytes of data.

15.2.3 Real-time Data Processing

While batch processing is useful for analyzing historical data, many AI applications require **real-time data processing**. For example, fraud detection systems, recommendation engines, and autonomous vehicles all need to process incoming data continuously.

- **Stream Processing with Spark Streaming**: Spark Streaming allows data to be processed in real-time as it arrives. It can be used to perform real-time analytics on data streams from sources like IoT devices, social media, or financial transactions.

Example: Streaming data processing with Spark

python

```
from pyspark.streaming import StreamingContext

# Set up Spark streaming context
ssc = StreamingContext(sparkContext, 1)  # 1 second batch interval

# Create DStream from a data source
stream_data = ssc.socketTextStream("localhost", 9999)  # Listening on port 9999

# Process data in real-time
stream_data.pprint()  # Print incoming data

ssc.start()  # Start the streaming context
```

ssc.awaitTermination() # Wait for termination

- **Lambda Architecture**: The **Lambda Architecture** is a popular model for real-time big data processing. It combines **batch processing** (Hadoop) for handling historical data and **real-time processing** (Spark Streaming) for analyzing incoming data. This hybrid approach ensures that large amounts of historical data can be processed alongside real-time events for timely insights.

15.3 Case Study: AI for Real-Time Data Analytics

Let's explore a real-world case study where we use AI for real-time data analytics. Suppose we are building an **IoT-based predictive maintenance system** for a manufacturing plant. The goal is to predict equipment failure in real-time to avoid costly downtime.

Step 1: Data Collection and Streaming

We have sensors embedded in the equipment that stream data continuously, including measurements like temperature, vibration, and pressure. These sensors send data to a central system (via **Kafka**, for example), which is processed in real-time using **Spark Streaming**.

python

```python
from pyspark.streaming import StreamingContext
from pyspark.sql import SparkSession

# Set up Spark context
spark = SparkSession.builder.appName('PredictiveMaintenance').getOrCreate()
ssc = StreamingContext(spark.sparkContext, 10)  # 10-second batch interval

# Read data stream (e.g., from Kafka)
stream_data = ssc.socketTextStream("localhost", 9999)

# Process the stream (e.g., calculate average temperature)
processed_data = stream_data.map(lambda x: float(x.split(',')[0]))  # Extract temperature data
processed_data.pprint()  # Print data for monitoring

ssc.start()
ssc.awaitTermination()
```

Step 2: Real-Time Model Prediction

Once the data is processed, we pass it through a trained machine learning model (e.g., a random forest classifier) to predict the likelihood of equipment failure. The model is continuously updated with new sensor data to improve its accuracy.

python

```
from pyspark.ml.classification import RandomForestClassificationModel

# Load pre-trained model
model = RandomForestClassificationModel.load("path_to_model")

# Predict failure risk in real-time
predictions = model.transform(processed_data)  # Use the processed data stream
predictions.pprint()  # Print predictions (failure risk)
```

Step 3: Real-Time Decision Making

Based on the model's predictions, real-time decisions can be made to alert maintenance staff or trigger automated systems to prevent failures. For example, if the model predicts a high likelihood of failure based on sensor readings, a maintenance ticket could be created automatically, and the equipment could be shut down for maintenance.

- **Big Data Frameworks**: Apache Spark and Hadoop are two of the most popular frameworks for processing large datasets. Spark is faster and more suited for real-time processing, while Hadoop is ideal for batch processing.

- **Data Preprocessing for Big Data**: Techniques such as data sampling, partitioning, and feature engineering are essential for preparing Big Data for AI and machine learning models.

- **Distributed Computing**: Big Data frameworks enable distributed processing, allowing AI models to scale across large datasets using multiple machines.

- **Real-time Data Processing**: Spark Streaming enables the processing of real-time data, making it possible to build applications like fraud detection systems, recommendation engines, and predictive maintenance systems.

- **AI for Real-Time Analytics**: By integrating AI models with real-time data pipelines, businesses can make informed decisions, improve operational efficiency, and prevent failures before they happen.

In this chapter, we've covered how to process, analyze, and apply machine learning models to Big Data using scalable and efficient frameworks like Spark and Hadoop. With these techniques, you can build AI-driven systems capable of making real-time predictions and decisions based on large, continuously flowing datasets.

CHAPTER 16: AI IN WEB AND MOBILE APPLICATIONS

In this chapter, we will explore how to integrate AI models into web and mobile applications. By embedding AI capabilities into these platforms, you can create smarter, more responsive applications that can interact with users and make decisions based on data in real-time. This chapter covers the integration of AI with web frameworks like **Flask** and **Django** for backend services, and outlines how to build AI-powered mobile applications using **TensorFlow Lite** or other lightweight solutions. We will conclude with a real-world use case where an AI-powered mobile application provides personalized recommendations to users.

16.1 Integrating AI Models into Web Applications

Web applications have become an essential part of modern software solutions. Integrating AI models into web apps enables businesses to provide dynamic, intelligent experiences to users. Whether it's recommending products, detecting fraud, or personalizing content, AI plays a critical role in enhancing the user experience.

16.1.1 Using Flask for Web Integration

Flask is a lightweight web framework in Python that is commonly used to build web applications. Flask provides the flexibility to easily integrate AI models and expose them through APIs or as part of the web application.

To integrate a machine learning model into a Flask web app:

1. **Train your AI model** (e.g., a scikit-learn model, a neural network in TensorFlow, or any other machine learning algorithm).

2. **Save the trained model** to disk using libraries like joblib (for scikit-learn models) or TensorFlow's Keras API for deep learning models.

3. **Expose the model** via an API endpoint in Flask, allowing web clients to interact with the model.

Example: Creating a Flask App with a Pre-trained Model

python

```python
from flask import Flask, request, jsonify
import joblib

app = Flask(__name__)

# Load pre-trained model
model = joblib.load('model.pkl')

@app.route('/predict', methods=['POST'])
def predict():
    # Get data from client request
    data = request.get_json(force=True)
    # Extract features from data
    features = [data['feature1'], data['feature2']]
    # Make prediction
    prediction = model.predict([features])
    # Return result as JSON
    return jsonify({'prediction': prediction[0]})

if __name__ == '__main__':
    app.run(debug=True)
```

In this example:

- We load a trained model using joblib.

- A /predict endpoint is created where clients can send data via POST requests to make predictions.

- The prediction is returned as a JSON response.

16.1.2 Using Django for Web Integration

Django is a more feature-rich web framework, ideal for building larger, more complex web applications. It includes many built-in tools such as authentication, database management, and form handling, making it a good choice when developing production-grade applications.

Integrating AI models with Django follows a similar approach as Flask:

1. **Model Integration**: You can integrate machine learning models into the Django views, either by loading the model at the start of the request or by storing the model in the database for efficient retrieval.

2. **APIs with Django Rest Framework**: For serving AI predictions via APIs, you can use the Django Rest Framework to expose machine learning models as endpoints.

Example: Django API for Model Prediction

python

```python
from django.http import JsonResponse
from rest_framework.decorators import api_view
import joblib

# Load the pre-trained model globally to avoid reloading on every request
model = joblib.load('model.pkl')

@api_view(['POST'])
def predict(request):
    data = request.data
    features = [data['feature1'], data['feature2']]
    prediction = model.predict([features])
    return JsonResponse({'prediction': prediction[0]})
```

In this Django example, the model is exposed via a REST API, and clients can make predictions by sending POST requests to the predict view.

16.2 Building AI-powered Mobile Applications

The rise of smartphones has opened up new opportunities for AI to be embedded in mobile applications. Whether for **personalized recommendations**, **face recognition**, or **real-time language translation**, AI can be integrated into mobile apps to improve user experience. However, mobile applications have different constraints (e.g., limited computational power and memory), so it's essential to optimize models for mobile use.

16.2.1 TensorFlow Lite for Mobile AI

TensorFlow Lite is a lightweight version of TensorFlow that is specifically designed for mobile and embedded devices. It allows you to deploy AI models on **Android** and **iOS** devices with optimized performance, ensuring that models run efficiently on mobile hardware.

Steps for Building an AI-powered Mobile App with TensorFlow Lite:

1. **Train the Model**: First, train your model using TensorFlow on your desktop or cloud machine. Once you have a trained model, you need to convert it to the TensorFlow Lite format.

2. **Convert the Model**: Use the TensorFlow Lite Converter to convert your model into a smaller, mobile-optimized version.

3. **Integrate with Mobile App**: Use the TensorFlow Lite Android or iOS SDKs to load the model and make predictions on mobile devices.

Example: Converting a Model to TensorFlow Lite

python

```python
import tensorflow as tf

# Load the trained model
model = tf.keras.models.load_model('model.h5')

# Convert the model to TensorFlow Lite format
```

```
converter = tf.lite.TFLiteConverter.from_keras_model(model)
tflite_model = converter.convert()


# Save the TFLite model to disk
with open('model.tflite', 'wb') as f:
    f.write(tflite_model)
```

This conversion process creates a .tflite file, which you can then integrate into your mobile application.

16.2.2 Mobile SDKs for AI

For **Android**, you can use the **TensorFlow Lite Android SDK**, while for **iOS**, the **TensorFlow Lite iOS SDK** allows you to load the .tflite model and make predictions. Additionally, many frameworks like **Core ML** (for iOS) and **ML Kit** (for Android) offer built-in AI tools that help integrate common AI tasks like image classification, object detection, and text recognition.

16.3 Real-World Use Case: AI-Powered Mobile App

Let's consider a real-world example where AI is integrated into a mobile app: **AI-powered personal health assistant**.

App Concept: Personal Health Assistant

The app collects health data from wearable devices (like heart rate, steps, sleep patterns) and provides personalized insights, such as:

- **Health status predictions** (e.g., the likelihood of developing a health condition).
- **Exercise suggestions** based on past activities.
- **Diet recommendations** tailored to user goals (e.g., weight loss or muscle gain).

Step 1: Collecting Data

The app collects data from wearable devices (via Bluetooth) or mobile sensors (e.g., accelerometer for tracking steps). This data is sent to the mobile app for processing.

Step 2: Model Training

The AI model is trained to predict user health status or provide recommendations based on historical data (e.g., heart rate trends, activity levels). This model could be a decision tree or a neural network.

Step 3: TensorFlow Lite Deployment

The trained model is converted to TensorFlow Lite format and integrated into the mobile app. This allows real-time predictions and insights directly on the user's device.

Step 4: Making Predictions

The app uses the TensorFlow Lite model to predict future health outcomes and provide personalized recommendations. For example, the app might predict that a user with consistent low activity levels might be at risk of obesity and suggest a customized workout plan.

- **Integrating AI into Web Applications**: Frameworks like **Flask** and **Django** can be used to serve AI models as REST APIs, enabling real-time predictions on web applications.

- **Mobile AI**: **TensorFlow Lite** enables you to deploy machine learning models on mobile devices, ensuring that models are optimized for performance and memory constraints.

- **AI-powered Mobile Apps**: Mobile applications can leverage AI to offer personalized experiences, from health assistants to recommendation engines. TensorFlow Lite and other mobile AI tools make it possible to embed AI capabilities into Android and iOS apps.

By the end of this chapter, you should be equipped to integrate AI models into both web and mobile applications, creating intelligent, data-driven user experiences.

CHAPTER 17: BUILDING INTELLIGENT CHATBOTS

Chatbots have evolved from simple scripted programs to sophisticated AI-driven systems capable of holding complex conversations with users. With the advent of **Natural Language Processing (NLP)** and **deep learning**, chatbots can now understand, generate, and respond to human language in more intuitive and context-aware ways. In this chapter, we will dive into how you can build an intelligent chatbot, starting with the fundamentals of NLP, training a chatbot using deep learning techniques, and examining a real-world case study of deploying a chatbot for customer service.

17.1 Natural Language Processing for Conversational AI

Natural Language Processing (NLP) is the field of AI concerned with enabling machines to understand and process human languages. NLP is the foundation for building conversational AI, as it allows chatbots to interpret user input (text or speech) and generate appropriate responses.

17.1.1 Key Concepts in NLP

1. **Tokenization**: This is the process of splitting a stream of text into words, phrases, or other meaningful units (tokens). Tokenization allows the system to break down text and process each part individually.

   Example:

   o Sentence: "I want to know the weather."

   o Tokens: ["I", "want", "to", "know", "the", "weather"]

2. **Named Entity Recognition (NER)**: NER is used to identify and classify entities in text (such as names, dates, locations, etc.). For a chatbot, understanding these entities can help personalize responses or direct users to the right information.

3. **Part-of-Speech (POS) Tagging**: This involves identifying the grammatical components of a sentence (e.g., noun, verb,

adjective) to understand the meaning and context of the sentence better.

4. **Intent Recognition**: The goal of intent recognition is to determine the user's goal from their input. For example, if a user types "What's the weather like today?", the intent is to retrieve weather information. Intent recognition is key to enabling chatbots to perform tasks.

5. **Word Embeddings**: Word embeddings (such as **Word2Vec** or **GloVe**) are vector representations of words that capture semantic meaning. These embeddings allow the model to understand not just the individual words but also their relationships with other words in context.

17.1.2 NLP Libraries for Chatbots

Several Python libraries can help with NLP tasks when building a chatbot. Some of the most popular ones include:

- **spaCy**: A fast and efficient NLP library that supports tokenization, POS tagging, NER, and more.

- **NLTK (Natural Language Toolkit)**: A comprehensive library for NLP tasks that includes tools for text processing, parsing, and classification.

- **Transformers (by Hugging Face)**: A library that provides pre-trained models for NLP tasks like sentiment analysis, question answering, and conversation generation. Models like **GPT-3** and **BERT** are part of this library, which can be directly used to build advanced conversational AI.

17.2 Training a Chatbot with Deep Learning

For a chatbot to be truly intelligent, it must be able to understand context, carry on a coherent conversation, and even handle multi-turn dialogues. This is where deep learning comes into play.

17.2.1 Sequence-to-Sequence Models (Seq2Seq)

The **Seq2Seq model** is one of the most common architectures for building conversational AI systems. It is based on **Recurrent Neural Networks (RNNs)**, particularly **Long Short-Term**

Memory (LSTM) networks, which are good at handling sequential data (like sentences or conversations).

A Seq2Seq model typically consists of:

1. **Encoder**: The encoder reads the input sentence (user's message) and encodes it into a fixed-length vector, which represents the sentence's meaning.

2. **Decoder**: The decoder then generates a response based on this encoded vector. The response is produced one word at a time, with each word dependent on the previous one.

Example: Building a Simple Seq2Seq Model with Keras

python

```
from tensorflow.keras.models import Sequential
from tensorflow.keras.layers import LSTM, Dense, Embedding

# Define a simple Seq2Seq model architecture
model = Sequential()
model.add(Embedding(input_dim=5000, output_dim=64))  # Embedding layer
model.add(LSTM(128, return_sequences=True))  # Encoder LSTM
```

```
model.add(LSTM(128))  # Decoder LSTM

model.add(Dense(5000, activation='softmax'))  # Output layer for word predictions


# Compile the model

model.compile(loss='categorical_crossentropy', optimizer='adam', metrics=['accuracy'])
```

In this basic example:

- The **Embedding layer** converts input words into dense vector representations.

- The **LSTM layers** process the sequences of words and encode the information.

- The **Dense layer** generates the output (the chatbot's response).

17.2.2 Pretrained Models and Transfer Learning

For more sophisticated chatbots, leveraging **pre-trained models** like **GPT-3** or **BERT** can significantly boost performance. These models are trained on vast amounts of data and have a deep understanding of language. Fine-tuning these models for your specific chatbot use case can be a great way to avoid training a model from scratch.

- **GPT-3**: A large transformer-based model by OpenAI that excels at text generation and can handle open-domain conversations.

- **BERT**: BERT is trained to understand the context of words in a sentence, making it useful for applications like question-answering, but it can also be fine-tuned for conversational tasks.

Using these models typically involves using the **Transformers library** from Hugging Face, which provides easy-to-use APIs to load and fine-tune these models.

Example: Using GPT-2 with Hugging Face

python

```
from transformers import GPT2LMHeadModel, GPT2Tokenizer
```

```
# Load pre-trained GPT-2 model and tokenizer
```

```
model = GPT2LMHeadModel.from_pretrained("gpt2")

tokenizer = GPT2Tokenizer.from_pretrained("gpt2")


# Tokenize input text

input_text = "Hello, how are you?"

input_ids = tokenizer.encode(input_text, return_tensors="pt")


# Generate a response

output = model.generate(input_ids, max_length=50, num_return_sequences=1)


# Decode the output

response = tokenizer.decode(output[0], skip_special_tokens=True)

print(response)
```

In this example:

- **GPT-2** generates a response based on the input query ("Hello, how are you?").

- The model is pre-trained, but you could further fine-tune it with domain-specific data to make the chatbot more relevant for your application.

17.3 Case Study: Deploying a Chatbot for Customer Service

Let's explore how to deploy a chatbot for customer service. The goal is to build a bot that can answer common customer queries, assist with order tracking, and provide recommendations based on customer preferences.

Step 1: Define Chatbot Scope and Use Cases

A customer service chatbot needs to handle specific use cases, such as:

- **Product inquiries**: "What is the price of product X?"
- **Order tracking**: "Where is my order?"
- **FAQ handling**: "How do I reset my password?"

Step 2: Collect Training Data

For a chatbot to handle these tasks, it needs training data. You can collect:

- **Frequently Asked Questions (FAQs)**: A list of common queries and responses.

- **Customer service interactions**: Data from real customer interactions can help train the model to understand real-world phrasing.

Step 3: Train the Chatbot

Using a sequence-to-sequence model or a pre-trained model like GPT-3, you can train the chatbot on your customer service data. For a more sophisticated system, you may use **intent recognition** to classify customer queries (e.g., "order status", "product info") and **entity extraction** to pull out relevant details (e.g., product name, order number).

Step 4: Deploying the Chatbot

To deploy the chatbot, you can:

1. **Integrate it with a website**: The chatbot can be deployed as a widget on your website using web technologies like **Flask**, **Django**, or **Node.js**.
2. **Integrate with messaging platforms**: Use APIs to integrate the chatbot with platforms like **Slack**, **Facebook Messenger**, or **WhatsApp**.

3. **Monitor and improve**: Once deployed, continually monitor the chatbot's performance and collect feedback to improve its responses over time.

Step 5: Post-Deployment Optimization

Even after deployment, it's important to continuously improve the chatbot's performance. This can be achieved through:

- **Active learning**: Collect feedback from users and retrain the model on this new data.

- **Human-in-the-loop**: For difficult cases, the chatbot can escalate the conversation to a human agent, learning from these interactions to improve future responses.

- **NLP for Chatbots**: Key NLP tasks such as tokenization, named entity recognition, and intent recognition are fundamental for building a chatbot that can understand user input and provide meaningful responses.

- **Deep Learning for Chatbots**: **Seq2Seq models** and **transformer-based models** like **GPT-3** and **BERT** are powerful tools for creating intelligent chatbots capable of engaging in real conversations.

- **Real-World Use Case**: Deploying a chatbot for customer service involves training a model on customer queries, defining use cases, and continuously improving the system post-deployment.

By the end of this chapter, you should have the foundational knowledge to start building your own intelligent chatbot and deploying it for real-world applications like customer support.

CHAPTER 18: ETHICS AND FAIRNESS IN AI

As artificial intelligence (AI) systems become more pervasive across industries, it is essential to understand the ethical implications and challenges they introduce. These challenges are not only about how AI is used but also about ensuring that the systems we create are fair, transparent, and accountable. This chapter delves into the **bias** inherent in AI models, the **ethical concerns** that arise with AI's integration into various applications, and strategies to promote fairness in AI.

18.1 Bias in AI Models and Mitigation Strategies

AI systems learn from data, and the data they are trained on often reflect human biases, historical inequalities, and societal prejudices. When these biases are not addressed, they can be perpetuated or even amplified by AI models. This section explores how bias can manifest in AI and how it can be mitigated.

18.1.1 Types of Bias in AI

1. **Data Bias**: Biases in the data can emerge from several sources, such as unrepresentative datasets, historical prejudices, or biased data collection methods. For example, if an AI model is trained on a dataset where certain demographics are underrepresented, the model may perform poorly for those groups.

    o **Example**: Facial recognition systems trained on a dataset predominantly containing white male faces might have higher error rates for women or people of color.

2. **Algorithmic Bias**: Even if the data is unbiased, the way an algorithm is structured or trained can introduce bias. Some algorithms may unintentionally prioritize certain features or patterns that lead to discriminatory outcomes.

    o **Example**: A credit scoring model might inadvertently discriminate against certain demographic groups if the features it uses (like zip code or income level) correlate with race or ethnicity.

3. **Measurement Bias**: This occurs when certain variables or features in the data are measured inaccurately or inconsistently. For instance, using outdated or flawed data sources for decision-making can create skewed results.

   o **Example**: Using self-reported data on income, where individuals from lower-income groups may underreport their earnings, leading to biased predictions in a loan application system.

18.1.2 Mitigation Strategies for Bias

Several strategies can be employed to detect, address, and mitigate bias in AI systems:

1. **Bias Detection**: It's important to audit AI models to identify and assess biases. Techniques like **Fairness Indicators** and **Disparate Impact Analysis** can help detect disparities in model performance across different demographic groups.

> ○ **Example**: In a hiring algorithm, a fairness audit can reveal whether the system is systematically disadvantaging applicants from certain age groups or ethnic backgrounds.

2. **Diverse Data**: Ensuring that the training data is diverse and representative of all relevant demographic groups is critical to avoiding bias. This can be done by **oversampling underrepresented groups** or **under-sampling overrepresented groups** in the training data to balance the model.

3. **Algorithmic Fairness Constraints**: Algorithms can be designed or modified to include fairness constraints. For example, in classification tasks, you can apply constraints to ensure that model decisions (e.g., predictions) are not biased across sensitive attributes (such as race, gender, or age).

> ○ **Example**: Fairness constraints can be integrated into a model's loss function to penalize any biased decision-making, ensuring that the algorithm treats all demographic groups equitably.

4. **Explainability and Transparency**: Ensuring that AI models are explainable and transparent allows stakeholders to understand how decisions are made, which can help uncover and mitigate bias. This can be achieved by using explainable AI techniques like **LIME** (Local Interpretable Model-Agnostic Explanations) and **SHAP** (SHapley Additive exPlanations).

  o **Example**: In a healthcare AI system, if a model recommends a treatment, using explainability tools can show whether the recommendation was influenced by factors such as race or gender.

5. **Bias Auditing**: Regular audits of AI systems post-deployment can help identify any emerging biases over time. Continual monitoring can ensure that models remain fair and equitable as they encounter new data.

18.2 Ethical Implications of AI in Real-World Applications

AI systems have the potential to significantly impact society, and with that comes a host of ethical challenges. As AI is integrated into more critical decision-making processes, it raises several questions related to fairness, privacy, accountability, and autonomy.

18.2.1 Fairness in Decision-Making

AI is increasingly being used in high-stakes applications like hiring, lending, criminal justice, and healthcare. In these contexts, the ethical implications of bias and fairness become especially pronounced.

- **Hiring**: AI tools are being used to filter resumes, assess candidates, and even conduct interviews. However, if these systems are trained on biased hiring data (e.g., favoring candidates of a particular gender or ethnic group), they can perpetuate discrimination. Companies need to ensure that their AI systems are transparent and do not unfairly disadvantage certain groups.

- **Lending**: AI models in the financial sector are used for credit scoring and loan approval. If these models are trained on historical lending data that reflects past discriminatory practices (e.g., giving fewer loans to minorities), they can continue to perpetuate inequality in financial services.

- **Criminal Justice**: Predictive policing algorithms and risk assessment tools used in criminal justice can have severe ethical consequences if they amplify biases against certain communities. For example, AI models used to predict the likelihood of reoffending may disproportionately label individuals from certain racial or socioeconomic backgrounds as high-risk.

18.2.2 Privacy Concerns

AI systems often require large amounts of personal data to function effectively. This raises serious concerns about privacy and data security. For example, facial recognition technology used in public spaces could lead to surveillance issues if data is not handled responsibly.

- **Example**: AI-powered social media platforms use personal data to recommend content. If the platform's algorithm collects excessive personal information without user consent, it could lead to privacy violations.

18.2.3 Accountability and Transparency

As AI systems become more autonomous, determining who is responsible when something goes wrong becomes a significant ethical concern. If an autonomous vehicle causes an accident or a healthcare AI makes an erroneous diagnosis, who is legally or ethically accountable? Ensuring transparency in AI decision-making processes and establishing clear accountability measures is critical to maintaining trust in AI systems.

18.2.4 Autonomy and Human Control

As AI systems become more capable, there are concerns about human autonomy. Autonomous systems, especially in areas like healthcare or law enforcement, may act without sufficient oversight or intervention. It's crucial that AI remains a tool that supports human decision-making rather than replacing it entirely.

- **Example**: In autonomous vehicles, the AI must be able to make real-time decisions in complex environments, but should always do so under the supervision and control of human operators in critical situations.

18.3 Case Studies of AI Fairness

18.3.1 Gender Bias in AI Recruitment Tools

One prominent example of AI bias in real-world applications is the **Amazon recruitment tool**, which was found to be biased against female candidates. The tool was trained on resumes submitted to Amazon over the past 10 years, which were predominantly from male candidates in technical roles. As a result, the AI system learned to prefer male candidates and penalized resumes with feminine language or female-associated keywords.

Mitigation: After the discovery, Amazon scrapped the tool, acknowledging that the data it had been trained on was biased. The incident underscores the importance of using diverse, representative training data and ensuring fairness when designing AI systems.

18.3.2 Predictive Policing and Racial Bias

PredPol, a predictive policing algorithm, was designed to predict where crimes were likely to occur, based on historical crime data. However, because the data used to train the algorithm reflected existing biases in the criminal justice system (e.g., over-policing certain neighborhoods), the system disproportionately targeted minority communities, reinforcing the cycle of discrimination.

Mitigation: Advocates for AI fairness argue for more transparent data collection, audits, and better alternatives to predictive policing, such as community-led crime prevention programs that take a more holistic approach to safety and justice.

18.3.3 AI in Healthcare: Radiology and Diagnostic Tools

In the field of healthcare, AI tools for diagnosing diseases (e.g., detecting cancerous tumors in medical imaging) have shown promise, but they have also raised fairness concerns. Some AI models trained on medical imaging datasets have been shown to have lower accuracy for patients from certain demographic groups, particularly for non-Caucasian patients, due to a lack of diverse training data.

Mitigation: Efforts are underway to ensure more diverse representation in healthcare datasets and to implement fairness-aware algorithms that can adapt to the needs of all patient groups, regardless of race, gender, or socioeconomic status.

- **Bias in AI**: AI models can inherit and amplify biases from training data. Strategies like diverse datasets, fairness constraints, and algorithmic audits can help mitigate these biases.

- **Ethical Implications**: AI systems can raise serious ethical concerns regarding fairness, privacy, accountability, and human control. These issues are especially critical in areas like hiring, criminal justice, and healthcare.

- **AI Fairness**: Real-world case studies, such as biased recruitment tools and predictive policing, illustrate the importance of building fair and transparent AI systems. Ongoing efforts are focused on improving the ethical design and deployment of AI technologies.

By the end of this chapter, you should have a solid understanding of the ethical challenges AI presents and the methods available to ensure fairness, transparency, and accountability in AI systems.

CHAPTER 19: AI FOR AUTONOMOUS SYSTEMS

Autonomous systems powered by artificial intelligence (AI) are revolutionizing industries ranging from transportation and logistics to agriculture and healthcare. These systems—ranging from self-driving cars to delivery drones—are capable of making decisions, performing tasks, and navigating environments without human intervention. In this chapter, we will explore the fundamentals of autonomous systems, focusing on **robotics, self-driving cars**, and **drone navigation systems**. We'll also look at how AI is used to enable these systems to function safely and efficiently in real-world environments.

19.1 Introduction to Robotics and Autonomous Systems

Robotics and **autonomous systems** are two fields closely linked with AI. While robotics involves the physical construction and operation of machines (robots), autonomous systems take this further by enabling these machines to operate independently, making decisions based on real-time data and pre-defined goals.

19.1.1 Key Concepts in Robotics and Autonomous Systems

1. **Sensors and Perception**: Autonomous systems rely heavily on sensors to gather information about their environment. Common sensors used in autonomous systems include:

    o **Cameras**: For visual input and image processing.

    o **LiDAR (Light Detection and Ranging)**: For creating 3D maps of the surroundings by measuring distances using laser light.

    o **Radar**: For detecting objects in low-visibility conditions (e.g., fog or rain).

    o **Ultrasonic sensors**: For close-range object detection.

The data from these sensors is processed and interpreted by AI algorithms to perceive the environment, identify obstacles, and make decisions.

2. **Path Planning**: Path planning refers to the process of determining an optimal path for the autonomous system to follow. This involves:

   o **Local path planning**: Calculating the best path in the immediate environment (e.g., avoiding obstacles).

   o **Global path planning**: Determining the best route from one point to another, considering long-term goals and constraints.

3. **Control Systems**: Once the autonomous system has made decisions about where to go or what to do, it needs control systems to execute those decisions. These systems ensure the robot or vehicle follows its path accurately and adjusts its actions based on environmental changes.

4. **Artificial Intelligence in Autonomous Systems**: AI plays a crucial role in enabling robots and autonomous systems to learn from experience and improve their performance. Techniques like **reinforcement learning** (RL) and **deep learning** (DL) are often employed to enable systems to adapt and refine their behaviors over time.

19.2 AI for Self-Driving Cars

Self-driving cars (also known as **autonomous vehicles** or AVs) represent one of the most ambitious applications of AI and robotics. These vehicles are designed to navigate the roads, interpret traffic signals, avoid obstacles, and make driving decisions without human intervention.

19.2.1 Key Technologies Behind Self-Driving Cars

1. **Computer Vision and Deep Learning**: Self-driving cars rely on computer vision to understand their surroundings. **Deep learning** algorithms are used to process data from cameras and sensors to recognize objects like pedestrians, other vehicles, traffic signs, and lane markings.

   o **Convolutional Neural Networks (CNNs)** are commonly used for image classification and object detection in self-driving cars.

2. **Sensor Fusion**: Self-driving cars use a combination of sensors like **LiDAR**, **radar**, and **cameras** to perceive their

environment. Sensor fusion refers to the technique of combining data from different sensors to create a more accurate and comprehensive understanding of the vehicle's surroundings.

- o For example, LiDAR provides precise distance measurements, while cameras provide rich visual data. Combining these data sources allows the car to detect obstacles in various weather conditions.

3. **Localization and Mapping**: To navigate the world, self-driving cars need to know their exact position on the road. **Localization** is the process of determining the vehicle's location using pre-built maps and real-time sensor data. This can involve **Simultaneous Localization and Mapping (SLAM)**, a technique that allows the car to create and update maps of its environment as it drives.

4. **Decision-Making and Planning**: The vehicle's AI system must decide how to respond to its environment. This includes **decision-making algorithms** that determine when to change lanes, stop at traffic lights, or yield to other

vehicles. These decisions are made using a combination of real-time sensor data, pre-programmed rules, and machine learning models that learn from experience.

- ○ **Reinforcement learning (RL)** is particularly useful for optimizing decision-making in complex, dynamic environments like road traffic.

5. **Safety and Testing**: One of the key challenges in self-driving cars is ensuring safety. Extensive testing in real-world conditions is necessary to ensure the vehicle can handle unexpected situations (e.g., pedestrians crossing the road, debris on the street, or inclement weather). AI models used in self-driving cars must be able to handle edge cases that might not be present in the training data.

19.2.2 Real-World Example: Waymo

Waymo, a subsidiary of Alphabet (Google's parent company), is one of the leaders in autonomous vehicle development. Waymo's self-driving cars use a combination of LiDAR, radar, cameras, and high-definition maps to navigate. The system relies heavily on deep learning for object detection, and reinforcement learning to make driving decisions.

Waymo cars have been tested extensively in multiple cities, covering millions of miles of driving data. This real-world testing is crucial for refining their AI models, improving decision-making algorithms, and handling rare or unexpected situations that occur on the road.

19.3 Real-World Application: Drone Navigation Systems

Drones, or **unmanned aerial vehicles (UAVs)**, are used in a wide variety of applications, including delivery, surveillance, agriculture, and infrastructure inspection. Similar to autonomous vehicles, drones need to navigate complex environments, avoid obstacles, and perform tasks autonomously.

19.3.1 Key Components of Drone Navigation Systems

1. **GPS and Localization**: Drones often use GPS to determine their position, but GPS alone can be unreliable in

environments with poor satellite visibility (e.g., indoors, urban canyons). As a result, drones often use a combination of **IMUs (Inertial Measurement Units)** and visual odometry to improve localization accuracy.

2. **Computer Vision for Obstacle Detection**: Just like autonomous cars, drones rely on computer vision to identify obstacles, such as trees, buildings, and power lines, in their flight path. Drones typically use **stereo cameras**, **LiDAR**, or **optical flow** to detect and avoid obstacles in real-time.

3. **Path Planning and Avoidance**: Drones must continuously plan their flight paths while avoiding obstacles. *A algorithm** and **RRT (Rapidly-exploring Random Trees)** are commonly used path planning techniques in drone navigation systems. These algorithms allow the drone to find optimal paths while considering obstacles and other constraints.

4. **Autonomous Flight Control**: Drones use a combination of AI and control systems to maintain stability and follow their flight path. AI-driven flight control systems are designed to

make real-time adjustments to the drone's speed, altitude, and orientation to ensure smooth, stable flight.

5. **Mission Planning**: Autonomous drones are often used for specific missions, such as surveying a region or delivering packages. AI systems allow drones to plan and execute complex missions autonomously, while continuously adjusting to dynamic environments (e.g., changing weather conditions or unexpected obstacles).

19.3.2 Real-World Example: DJI Drones

DJI, a leader in consumer and commercial drone technology, has integrated AI into its drone systems for a wide range of functionalities. Their drones are equipped with advanced computer vision algorithms that enable features like **Obstacle Avoidance**, **ActiveTrack (tracking moving objects)**, and **Smart Return to Home (RTH)**. These AI-driven features allow drones to navigate autonomously and avoid obstacles while following a predefined route.

DJI's drones use a combination of visual sensors and LiDAR to map the environment, allowing them to fly safely in both indoor and outdoor environments. Their advanced flight control systems use real-time AI to adjust to changing conditions, such as wind or sudden obstacles.

19.4 Challenges and Future Directions for Autonomous Systems

1. **Ethical and Legal Concerns**: Autonomous systems, especially self-driving cars, raise important ethical and legal questions. For example, who is responsible if an autonomous vehicle causes an accident? How do we ensure that these systems are making decisions that align with human values and ethics?

2. **Regulation and Safety Standards**: Governments around the world are developing regulations and safety standards to govern the development and deployment of autonomous systems. Ensuring the safety and reliability of these systems

is critical, particularly in high-risk environments like transportation.

3. **AI Robustness and Generalization**: While AI models have made significant strides, autonomous systems still face challenges related to robustness and generalization. In unpredictable environments (e.g., a new city for a self-driving car or a storm for a drone), these systems must be able to adapt in real-time.

- **Robotics and Autonomous Systems**: These systems combine AI, sensors, control algorithms, and path planning techniques to perform tasks autonomously. AI helps these systems understand and interact with the environment to make intelligent decisions.

- **Self-Driving Cars**: Self-driving cars use AI to navigate the road, make decisions, and adapt to dynamic environments. Key technologies include computer vision, sensor fusion, reinforcement learning, and path planning.

- **Drone Navigation**: Drones use a combination of GPS, computer vision, and path planning algorithms to navigate complex environments autonomously. AI is used to enable features like obstacle avoidance and mission planning.

- **Challenges**: Ethical, legal, and safety concerns remain significant challenges for the widespread adoption of autonomous systems.

This chapter provides a foundation for understanding the role of AI in autonomous systems. As these technologies continue to evolve, they will shape the future of industries such as transportation, logistics, and robotics. By understanding the principles and challenges discussed here, you are better equipped to work with AI-driven autonomous systems in real-world applications.

CHAPTER 20: AI IN HEALTHCARE

Artificial intelligence (AI) is making a profound impact on healthcare, offering new ways to diagnose diseases, personalize treatment plans, and predict health outcomes. AI's ability to process vast amounts of medical data, learn from patterns, and improve over time is transforming clinical workflows, enhancing patient care, and enabling more precise and timely interventions. This chapter explores the role of AI in healthcare, focusing on **predictive models**, **AI applications in diagnostics and treatment**, and **medical image analysis**.

20.1 Predictive Models for Healthcare

Predictive models use AI and machine learning algorithms to analyze historical data and make predictions about future events. In healthcare, these models are used to predict disease risk, forecast patient outcomes, and guide clinical decision-making. By analyzing large datasets, including medical records, lab results, and patient histories, AI can identify patterns that may be invisible to human clinicians.

20.1.1 Key Applications of Predictive Models in Healthcare

1. **Predicting Disease Risk**: Predictive models are increasingly used to assess the risk of diseases such as heart disease, diabetes, and cancer. By examining patient demographics, lifestyle factors, family history, and past medical conditions, AI systems can predict which individuals are at higher risk and recommend preventive measures.

   o **Example**: A machine learning model that analyzes a patient's medical history, lifestyle choices, and genetic data to predict the likelihood of developing diabetes. Early intervention strategies can then be implemented, such as lifestyle changes or regular monitoring.

2. **Early Detection and Diagnosis**: Predictive models help identify the early signs of diseases that may not yet show clinical symptoms. For example, models that analyze medical records and diagnostic data can predict the

likelihood of conditions such as sepsis, which can be fatal if not caught early.

- o **Example**: AI-based systems used in **early detection of cancer** can analyze a patient's lab results and imaging data to identify abnormal cell patterns indicative of early-stage cancer, leading to timely intervention and improved survival rates.

3. **Patient Outcome Prediction**: AI models are used to predict patient outcomes, such as the likelihood of recovery, disease progression, or complications. These models can help clinicians tailor treatment plans based on predicted outcomes, improving patient management and care.

- o **Example**: A predictive model used in intensive care units (ICUs) to monitor patients' vital signs in real time and predict which patients are at risk of developing life-threatening conditions, enabling clinicians to act preemptively.

20.1.2 Building Predictive Models in Healthcare

Predictive models in healthcare are typically built using machine learning algorithms, such as **logistic regression**, **decision trees**, **random forests**, and **neural networks**. These models are trained on large datasets of patient information and outcomes.

- **Data Preparation**: The data used to train these models must be cleaned and preprocessed, with missing values addressed and relevant features (such as patient demographics, medical histories, lab results) carefully selected. Feature engineering and data normalization are important steps in improving model accuracy.

- **Model Evaluation**: Evaluating predictive models requires using metrics such as **accuracy, precision, recall, F1-score**, and **AUC (Area Under the Curve)** to assess their effectiveness. These metrics help ensure the model is reliable and suitable for real-world clinical use.

- **Real-World Considerations**: Models must be designed to handle the challenges of medical data, such as **imbalanced**

datasets (e.g., where some conditions are much rarer than others) and the **high variability** of patient populations.

20.2 AI Applications in Diagnostics and Treatment

AI's ability to analyze medical data quickly and accurately makes it a powerful tool in diagnostic procedures and treatment planning. From automated analysis of lab results to personalized treatment recommendations, AI applications in diagnostics and treatment are improving efficiency and outcomes in healthcare.

20.2.1 AI in Diagnostics

1. **Medical Image Analysis**: AI has made significant strides in the analysis of medical images, enabling more accurate and faster diagnoses. AI systems, particularly those based on **deep learning** (e.g., convolutional neural networks or CNNs), are now capable of detecting abnormalities in medical images, such as X-rays, MRIs, CT scans, and ultrasounds.

- o **Example**: AI models that analyze mammograms to detect early signs of breast cancer, or models that can identify **tumors** in CT scans of the brain, helping radiologists identify issues faster and with greater accuracy.

2. **Laboratory Diagnostics**: AI is also being applied to laboratory diagnostics, where machine learning algorithms analyze blood tests, genetic data, and other biomarkers to provide diagnostic insights. AI can detect patterns in lab results that may not be obvious to a human doctor, helping to identify conditions at an early stage.

   - o **Example**: AI tools that analyze genetic testing results to identify mutations associated with diseases like cancer, enabling personalized treatment plans based on the genetic makeup of the individual.

3. **Natural Language Processing (NLP) for Medical Records**: AI systems using **NLP** can read and interpret unstructured data from clinical notes and medical records.

This helps clinicians to extract key insights, making the diagnostic process more efficient.

- o **Example**: NLP algorithms that scan a patient's medical history for key symptoms or risk factors that might indicate a developing condition, providing clinicians with timely alerts.

20.2.2 AI in Treatment

1. **Personalized Medicine**: AI is helping to create personalized treatment plans by analyzing a patient's genetic information, lifestyle data, and medical history to recommend the most effective treatments. This approach ensures that patients receive the right treatment tailored to their specific needs, rather than relying on generalized treatment protocols.

   - o **Example**: AI algorithms that analyze genetic mutations to recommend personalized cancer treatments, identifying drugs that are more likely to be effective based on the patient's genetic profile.

2. **Drug Discovery and Development**: AI is accelerating drug discovery by analyzing biological data, identifying potential drug targets, and simulating how drugs interact with the body. This can dramatically reduce the time and cost of developing new drugs.

   o **Example**: AI tools that predict how potential new drugs will interact with specific proteins in the body, aiding pharmaceutical companies in discovering promising new treatments faster.

3. **Clinical Decision Support Systems (CDSS)**: AI-based clinical decision support systems assist healthcare providers in making better clinical decisions. These systems use patient data to suggest possible diagnoses, recommend treatments, and alert clinicians to potential risks.

   o **Example**: An AI system that suggests treatment plans for a patient with a rare disease, based on an analysis of similar cases from a global database of medical records.

ARTIFICIAL INTELLIGENCE WITH PYTHON

4. **Robotic Surgery**: AI-driven robotic surgery systems assist surgeons by providing real-time data and precision during operations. These systems can analyze patient data and offer suggestions on the best surgical techniques to minimize risks and improve recovery times.

   o **Example**: A robotic system that uses AI to perform minimally invasive procedures, with a surgeon providing oversight and guidance. The system may adjust the surgical tools automatically based on the patient's anatomy and real-time feedback.

20.3 Case Study: AI for Medical Image Analysis

Medical image analysis is one of the most promising areas for AI in healthcare, with numerous applications across various specialties, including radiology, oncology, ophthalmology, and dermatology. This section focuses on a case study of AI's impact on **medical image analysis**, particularly in the context of **radiology**.

20.3.1 Use of AI in Radiology

In radiology, AI-powered systems are used to assist in the interpretation of medical images. These systems use deep learning techniques, such as **CNNs**, to analyze images and detect abnormalities, such as tumors, fractures, or signs of disease.

- **Example**: AI algorithms that analyze chest X-rays to detect **pneumonia, lung cancer**, or **tuberculosis**. These systems are trained on large datasets of medical images, enabling them to recognize subtle patterns that may be difficult for human radiologists to identify.

- **Real-World Impact**: In a clinical trial, an AI system developed by **Google Health** achieved diagnostic accuracy in breast cancer detection that surpassed human radiologists. The system analyzed mammograms and identified malignancies with higher sensitivity and fewer false positives than human experts.

20.3.2 Workflow and Efficiency

AI in medical imaging can enhance efficiency by **automating routine tasks**, such as image segmentation (identifying areas of interest in an image), which can save radiologists significant time. AI also improves **diagnostic accuracy** by providing second opinions, reducing the likelihood of missed diagnoses and minimizing human error.

- **Example**: An AI system that automatically segments brain MRI scans to highlight areas of concern, such as lesions or tumors. Radiologists can then focus their attention on these areas, improving diagnostic accuracy and reducing the time needed for analysis.

20.3.3 Challenges and Considerations

1. **Data Quality**: AI models require high-quality, diverse datasets to train effectively. Medical images must be annotated accurately, and models must be exposed to a wide range of cases to generalize effectively across populations.

2. **Regulatory Approval**: AI systems in healthcare must undergo rigorous testing and validation to ensure their safety and effectiveness. In many countries, AI tools for medical

image analysis require regulatory approval before they can be used in clinical settings.

3. **Integration with Clinical Workflows**: For AI systems to be truly effective, they must be integrated seamlessly into the existing clinical workflows. This includes ensuring that AI tools are easy for healthcare providers to use and that they complement human expertise.

- **Predictive Models**: AI is used to predict disease risk, patient outcomes, and identify early signs of conditions. These models help clinicians make better, data-driven decisions.

- **AI in Diagnostics**: AI applications in medical diagnostics, including medical image analysis and laboratory tests, enable faster and more accurate diagnoses.

- **AI in Treatment**: AI supports personalized medicine, drug discovery, and clinical decision-making, improving treatment plans and patient outcomes.

- **Medical Image Analysis**: AI, particularly deep learning, is transforming medical imaging by enhancing diagnostic accuracy, automating routine tasks, and improving clinical workflows.

- **Challenges**: Issues such as data quality, regulatory approval, and integration into clinical practice must be addressed to ensure the successful implementation of AI in healthcare.

AI's potential to improve healthcare is vast, but successful deployment requires careful consideration of ethical, practical, and regulatory challenges. By combining AI with human expertise, healthcare providers can offer better, more personalized care to patients, improving health outcomes and reducing costs.

CHAPTER 21: AI FOR FINANCE AND BUSINESS

Artificial intelligence is rapidly reshaping the financial and business sectors by enabling smarter decision-making, improving operational efficiency, and providing insights that were once out of reach. From **financial forecasting** to **fraud detection** and **algorithmic trading**, AI is becoming an indispensable tool for businesses looking to stay competitive and optimize performance. This chapter explores key AI applications in finance and business, focusing on how AI is transforming industries, along with a real-world case study on AI for business decision-making.

21.1 AI Applications in Financial Forecasting

In the financial sector, forecasting is essential for making informed decisions about investments, managing risks, and predicting market trends. AI-powered tools, especially those based on machine learning and deep learning, are capable of analyzing vast amounts of financial data to make more accurate predictions and uncover hidden patterns.

21.1.1 Key Applications of AI in Financial Forecasting

1. **Stock Market Prediction**: AI models, particularly **time series forecasting** algorithms, are used to predict stock prices, currency exchange rates, and commodity prices. These models analyze historical data, such as past prices, trading volumes, and economic indicators, to forecast future market trends.

   o **Example**: Machine learning models that predict stock market trends by analyzing historical price data, news sentiment, and social media discussions. These models can offer buy or sell recommendations based on trends and sentiment analysis, improving investment strategies.

2. **Risk Management**: AI-driven risk models can help financial institutions assess the risk of investments, loans, and other financial instruments. By analyzing multiple

factors, including market conditions, credit history, and economic indicators, these models identify potential risks and suggest mitigation strategies.

- ○ **Example**: A bank using AI to assess the risk of a loan applicant by analyzing their credit history, income, spending patterns, and broader economic trends. This predictive model helps reduce defaults by ensuring that loans are granted to individuals who can repay them.

3. **Revenue Forecasting**: Businesses use AI for forecasting revenues by analyzing historical sales data, consumer behavior, seasonal patterns, and macroeconomic trends. AI can identify trends that might not be immediately obvious, helping businesses plan for future growth and adjust their strategies accordingly.

- ○ **Example**: An AI system used by a retail company to forecast future revenue based on customer purchasing behavior, seasonal sales patterns, and broader economic data. These predictions help the company optimize inventory and sales strategies.

21.1.2 Techniques in Financial Forecasting

1. **Time Series Analysis**: Time series models, such as **ARIMA (AutoRegressive Integrated Moving Average)** and **LSTM (Long Short-Term Memory)** networks, are often used for forecasting financial data. These models take into account the historical values of a time series to predict future data points.

2. **Machine Learning Algorithms**: **Random Forests, Gradient Boosting Machines (GBM)**, and **Support Vector Machines (SVMs)** are common machine learning algorithms used for financial forecasting. These models work by identifying patterns in complex, multi-dimensional datasets, improving the accuracy of predictions.

3. **Deep Learning Models**: **Neural networks**, especially **Recurrent Neural Networks (RNNs)** and **LSTMs**, are frequently used in forecasting financial data. These models

are particularly effective at learning from sequential data (like stock prices) and can account for temporal dependencies.

21.2 Fraud Detection, Algorithmic Trading, and Credit Scoring

AI is also widely used for combating fraud, improving trading strategies, and making credit decisions. These applications leverage AI's ability to detect anomalies, recognize patterns, and make predictions based on large volumes of financial data.

21.2.1 Fraud Detection

Fraud detection in finance relies on AI's ability to detect unusual patterns and anomalies that could indicate fraudulent activities. Machine learning models are trained on historical transaction data to recognize behaviors that deviate from normal patterns, flagging potential fraud in real time.

- **Example**: AI-powered fraud detection systems used by credit card companies to identify unusual transactions. By analyzing factors such as transaction size, location, and purchase history, the system can identify potentially fraudulent activity and alert the cardholder or block the transaction.

21.2.2 Algorithmic Trading

Algorithmic trading involves using AI algorithms to execute high-frequency trades based on predefined conditions. These algorithms can analyze large datasets in real time and execute trades at speeds and frequencies that humans cannot match. AI-powered trading systems can adapt to market conditions, optimizing trading strategies based on the latest data.

- **Example**: An AI-driven algorithmic trading system that analyzes stock price movements, economic news, and social media sentiment in real time. The system uses this information to execute buy or sell orders at optimal times, aiming to maximize profits and minimize losses.

21.2.3 Credit Scoring

AI is increasingly used in credit scoring to provide more accurate assessments of an individual's creditworthiness. Traditional credit scores rely on a limited set of criteria, such as credit history and income, but AI models can incorporate a broader range of factors, such as social media activity, spending behavior, and even psychometric data.

- **Example**: An AI-based credit scoring model used by a fintech company to assess the creditworthiness of individuals who may not have a traditional credit history. The model analyzes a variety of alternative data sources, such as payment history, transaction behavior, and even mobile phone usage, to provide a more accurate picture of an individual's financial reliability.

21.3 Real-World Example: AI for Business Decision-Making

AI is also revolutionizing decision-making in businesses across various industries. By analyzing data from operations, marketing, finance, and customer service, AI models can provide executives with insights that support better, faster decision-making.

1. **Customer Segmentation**: AI tools analyze customer data (e.g., demographics, behavior, purchasing patterns) to segment customers into distinct groups. This allows businesses to target specific customer segments with personalized marketing campaigns, improving conversion rates and customer retention.

   o **Example**: An e-commerce platform using AI to segment its customer base based on buying patterns and preferences. The platform then tailors marketing messages to different customer segments, resulting in higher engagement and sales.

2. **Demand Forecasting**: AI-driven demand forecasting systems analyze historical sales data, seasonality, and market trends to predict future demand for products or

services. This helps businesses optimize inventory levels, pricing strategies, and promotional efforts.

- o **Example**: A retailer using AI to forecast demand for products during a specific season. By analyzing historical sales, weather data, and consumer trends, the company can better manage inventory and avoid overstocking or understocking products.

21.3.2 AI in Human Resources (HR)

AI is also transforming human resources by streamlining recruitment processes, improving employee performance management, and fostering a more diverse and inclusive workplace.

1. **Recruitment**: AI can screen resumes, match candidates to job descriptions, and even assess candidates' skills through automated tests. This reduces the time and cost associated with hiring and helps companies identify the best candidates more efficiently.

   - o **Example**: A company using AI to automatically screen resumes for job openings, ranking candidates based on how well their qualifications match the job requirements. The system can also identify keywords and evaluate whether the candidate's background aligns with company culture.

2. **Employee Retention**: AI-powered analytics can identify patterns in employee behavior that predict turnover, helping companies take proactive steps to retain top talent. These systems analyze factors such as job satisfaction, work performance, and employee engagement to predict which employees are most likely to leave.

   o **Example**: A company using AI to monitor employee engagement surveys, work performance data, and internal communications to identify signs of dissatisfaction. The system helps HR teams intervene before employees decide to leave.

21.3.3 AI for Strategic Decision-Making

AI provides decision-makers with powerful tools to make more informed strategic decisions. By analyzing vast amounts of data, AI systems can uncover trends, forecast future outcomes, and suggest optimal strategies.

- **Example**: A company analyzing customer feedback, sales data, and market trends using AI to make decisions about product development. The AI model identifies opportunities for new products based on unmet customer needs and changing market conditions.

AI is fundamentally transforming the way businesses operate, from financial forecasting and fraud detection to marketing, sales, and human resources. By leveraging AI's ability to analyze vast amounts of data and uncover hidden patterns, businesses can make more accurate predictions, optimize processes, and make smarter decisions.

In finance, AI is revolutionizing risk management, stock market prediction, and credit scoring, enabling financial institutions to stay competitive while reducing risks. In business, AI tools are helping companies make more informed strategic decisions, improve customer experiences, and streamline operations. As AI continues to evolve, its impact on finance and business will only grow, providing new opportunities for innovation and growth.

By understanding the capabilities and applications of AI in these industries, you are better equipped to leverage AI in your own work, whether you're making financial decisions, improving business processes, or developing AI-driven solutions for real-world challenges.

CHAPTER 22: AI SECURITY AND PRIVACY

As artificial intelligence continues to be integrated into everyday applications across industries, its security and privacy implications have become paramount. While AI can enhance the effectiveness of cybersecurity systems, it also introduces new challenges. From **AI in cybersecurity** to the need for safeguarding AI models against **adversarial attacks** and managing **privacy concerns**, this chapter explores the key security issues surrounding AI technologies and highlights techniques for ensuring the integrity and confidentiality of AI systems.

22.1 AI in Cybersecurity

AI has become a critical tool in enhancing cybersecurity. By leveraging AI to analyze vast amounts of data, detect anomalies, and respond to threats, organizations can improve their security posture and reduce the risk of breaches. AI can automate many of the tasks traditionally carried out by security teams, providing faster response times and more accurate threat detection.

22.1.1 Key Applications of AI in Cybersecurity

1. **Threat Detection and Prevention**: AI can identify unusual patterns in network traffic or system behavior, which may indicate a cyberattack. By analyzing large datasets of system logs and user activities, AI algorithms can detect potential threats, such as malware, ransomware, or phishing attempts, in real time.

    o   **Example**: AI-based intrusion detection systems (IDS) that use **machine learning** to analyze network traffic. These systems can recognize the typical behavior of network activity and flag any deviation as potentially malicious, such as a sudden spike in data transfer or unauthorized login attempts.

2. **Anomaly Detection**: Machine learning algorithms are excellent at identifying **anomalous behavior** within systems, networks, or applications. By learning from historical data,

AI can detect activities that do not align with established patterns, allowing for early detection of attacks.

- o **Example**: An AI model that monitors access patterns to a company's financial database. If a user who typically only accesses certain files suddenly begins downloading large amounts of sensitive data, the AI system will trigger an alert for a potential data breach or insider threat.

3. **Automated Response to Cyberattacks**: AI systems can automate responses to detected threats, such as isolating compromised machines, blocking suspicious IP addresses, or quarantining affected files. This reduces the response time and helps mitigate attacks before they cause significant damage.

- o **Example**: In the event of a ransomware attack, an AI-powered system could automatically isolate affected devices from the network, preventing the spread of the ransomware and buying time for security teams to mitigate the threat.

4. **Phishing Detection**: AI is widely used in detecting phishing attacks by analyzing email content, website URLs, and user behavior. Machine learning models trained on vast datasets of phishing and non-phishing emails can help identify fraudulent messages with high accuracy.

   o **Example**: An AI-based email filter that scans incoming messages for signs of phishing attempts, such as suspicious links, unusual sender addresses, or the use of urgency tactics. The system then flags these emails as potential threats or warns users of possible phishing attempts.

22.1.2 Challenges in Using AI for Cybersecurity

- **Data Quality and Availability**: For AI systems to be effective in detecting threats, they require high-quality, labeled datasets. Collecting and labeling data from diverse threat scenarios can be challenging, especially in rapidly evolving cyberattacks.

- **False Positives**: Machine learning models, especially in anomaly detection, can generate false positives—flagging legitimate activities as suspicious. These can overwhelm security teams and may lead to missed or delayed responses to real threats.

- **Evolving Threat Landscape**: Cyberattacks are continuously evolving, and adversaries are becoming more sophisticated in their strategies. AI systems must be able to adapt quickly to detect new attack vectors and behaviors, which requires ongoing updates and model retraining.

22.2 Protecting AI Models from Adversarial Attacks

While AI is increasingly being used for cybersecurity, AI models themselves are vulnerable to **adversarial attacks**. These attacks involve manipulating the input data to deceive an AI model into making incorrect predictions or classifications. Adversarial attacks can be used to bypass security systems, mislead autonomous vehicles, or corrupt decision-making systems.

22.2.1 What are Adversarial Attacks?

Adversarial attacks typically involve small, carefully crafted perturbations to input data that cause the AI model to misinterpret the data. In image recognition, for example, adversarial noise might be added to an image in such a way that the model misclassifies it, while a human observer would see no difference.

- **Example**: In a self-driving car, an adversarial attack could modify the road signs in such a way that the car's image recognition system misinterprets a stop sign as a yield sign, leading to a dangerous situation.

22.2.2 Types of Adversarial Attacks

1. **Evasion Attacks**: These attacks are aimed at deceiving the AI model at the time of decision-making. The attacker modifies the input data to evade detection or misclassification without necessarily affecting the underlying data source.

○ **Example**: A malware detection system trained with AI can be evaded by embedding malware code in legitimate files. The attacker carefully crafts the code so that it passes undetected by the AI system.

2. **Poisoning Attacks**: In poisoning attacks, the attacker introduces malicious data into the training set to corrupt the learning process. This results in a model that is biased or inaccurate, which may then make incorrect predictions or decisions in real-world scenarios.

○ **Example**: If an attacker can inject malicious labels into a training dataset for a spam email filter, the model might learn to misclassify benign emails as spam or vice versa.

3. **Model Inversion Attacks**: These attacks aim to extract sensitive information from the AI model itself. By querying the model with carefully crafted inputs, an attacker can reverse-engineer the model to reveal confidential data it was trained on, such as private user information.

o **Example**: An adversary could use model inversion techniques on a facial recognition system to retrieve personal information about individuals who are part of the model's training data.

22.2.3 Techniques for Defending Against Adversarial Attacks

1. **Adversarial Training**: One of the most common defense strategies is to augment the training data with adversarial examples. By training the AI model on both normal and adversarial examples, the model becomes more robust to attacks and can correctly classify perturbed inputs.

2. **Defensive Distillation**: This technique involves training a model to output softer probabilities (instead of hard classifications), making it more resistant to small perturbations in the input data. Distilled models have been shown to be more resistant to adversarial inputs.

3. **Input Data Sanitization**: In this approach, the input data is preprocessed to remove potential adversarial perturbations before it is fed into the model. This can involve filtering out

suspicious data, detecting anomalies, or applying techniques such as **denoising** to clean input data.

4. **Ensemble Methods**: Using multiple models, or an ensemble, to make predictions can help reduce the vulnerability to adversarial attacks. By combining the outputs of several models, the chances of an attacker succeeding in manipulating the outcome of the system are reduced.

22.3 Privacy Concerns and Techniques in AI

AI systems often require access to vast amounts of personal and sensitive data to function effectively. This raises significant privacy concerns, especially in sectors such as healthcare, finance, and retail. In these cases, it is crucial to protect user data while still enabling AI systems to provide value.

22.3.1 Key Privacy Concerns in AI

1. **Data Collection and Use**: AI systems often require massive datasets to train, which may include personally identifiable

information (PII) or sensitive data. The collection, storage, and use of this data must comply with privacy laws such as **GDPR** (General Data Protection Regulation) and **CCPA** (California Consumer Privacy Act), which impose strict rules on how personal data can be handled.

2. **Data Sharing**: AI systems that rely on shared data or data collected from multiple sources may inadvertently expose private information. This is especially a concern in industries like healthcare, where sensitive patient data is involved.

3. **Model Inversion and Membership Inference**: As mentioned earlier, adversarial attacks like **model inversion** can reveal private data that AI models have been trained on. In addition, **membership inference attacks** aim to determine whether a specific data point was part of the model's training set, potentially exposing sensitive information.

22.3.2 Techniques for Ensuring Privacy in AI

1. **Differential Privacy**: Differential privacy is a technique used to ensure that individual data points cannot be identified in aggregated data. It adds random noise to the data or the results of queries to obscure any specific individual's information, protecting privacy while still allowing the model to learn useful patterns.

   o **Example**: A company might use differential privacy to train a machine learning model on customer data without risking exposure of any specific individual's data, ensuring that even if the model is queried, it does not reveal any private information.

2. **Federated Learning**: Federated learning is a decentralized approach where the training of the AI model occurs across multiple devices or locations without sharing the actual data. Only model updates, rather than raw data, are shared, preserving the privacy of individual data sources.

   o **Example**: In a federated learning setup for healthcare, AI models can be trained on patient data stored locally in hospitals or clinics. The model updates are then shared with a central server for aggregation, without the need to transfer sensitive patient data.

3. **Homomorphic Encryption**: Homomorphic encryption allows data to be processed in an encrypted form, meaning that data can be analyzed and modeled without ever decrypting it. This ensures that sensitive data remains private even when it is being used by AI systems.

   o **Example**: A healthcare provider could use homomorphic encryption to process encrypted patient data in an AI model, allowing for analytics to be performed without exposing private medical information.

AI's integration into cybersecurity and its impact on privacy are two of the most critical areas of concern in the evolving AI landscape. As AI continues to enhance security measures, such as threat detection and automated responses to cyberattacks, it also faces new challenges, particularly with regard to adversarial attacks and privacy risks. Ensuring the security and privacy of AI systems requires ongoing vigilance, the adoption of robust defense mechanisms, and compliance with privacy regulations.

By understanding both the opportunities and risks AI introduces in security and privacy, organizations can better protect their AI systems, users, and data, fostering trust and maximizing the potential of AI to improve cybersecurity and safeguard personal privacy.

CHAPTER 23: SCALING AI MODELS FOR PRODUCTION

Deploying AI models into production is one of the most complex and critical stages in the AI development lifecycle. It's one thing to build a machine learning or deep learning model in a controlled environment, but when transitioning to real-world applications, scaling and maintaining these models across a large infrastructure becomes a significant challenge. This chapter delves into the best practices for deploying AI models at scale, discusses the use of cloud services to facilitate this process, and walks through a case study on building an AI product from prototype to full-scale production.

23.1 Deploying AI Models at Scale

Deploying an AI model at scale involves not only making sure that the model performs well on a single instance but also ensuring it can handle a large volume of data, high traffic, and diverse use cases across multiple environments. Scaling AI models requires careful consideration of both **technical infrastructure** and **operational workflows**.

23.1.1 Key Considerations for Scaling AI Models

1. **Model Performance and Latency**: As AI models are deployed at scale, performance becomes a key concern. In production, models need to respond quickly (low latency) and accurately, even when faced with large datasets or heavy traffic. Depending on the use case, performance can be prioritized differently—for instance, real-time applications like autonomous driving require extremely low latency, while batch processing applications (e.g., fraud detection) may be more tolerant of latency.

   o **Example**: A recommendation system for an e-commerce platform must be able to provide personalized suggestions in real-time without compromising the speed of the website or app. This might involve serving the model from a distributed network of servers and optimizing it for low-latency inference.

2. **Scalability and Infrastructure**: Ensuring that the infrastructure can handle increased load is crucial. This typically involves scaling the **compute resources** (e.g., GPUs, TPUs) and **storage** (e.g., data lakes, distributed file systems) horizontally across multiple servers or cloud instances. It's essential to automate scaling, such that as traffic increases, the system can scale up resources without manual intervention.

   o **Example**: A video streaming platform using AI for content recommendations would need to scale its model across thousands of servers to handle millions of user interactions simultaneously. The system should be able to automatically scale based on user demand and resource consumption.

3. **Model Versioning and Updates**: In production, models need to be continuously monitored and updated to ensure they remain accurate and relevant. This involves managing

model versioning (i.e., tracking different versions of the model), rolling out updates without downtime, and ensuring that new versions do not disrupt user experience.

- o **Example**: A financial institution deploying AI to assess loan applications may release regular updates to its model to account for changing economic conditions. Versioning ensures that the new model is properly tested before being deployed to replace the previous version.

4. **Monitoring and Logging**: Continuous monitoring is critical to ensure that the AI model performs as expected. This includes tracking its accuracy, latency, and resource usage, as well as identifying **drift** (i.e., when the model's performance degrades due to changes in the underlying data). It's also essential to log every prediction and model input/output for auditing and debugging purposes.

- o **Example**: In a machine learning-driven fraud detection system, logs can help track flagged transactions, allowing the team to review model performance and make adjustments as needed. Logs also help in understanding why a model might make certain predictions, aiding in debugging.

23.2 Cloud Services for AI

Cloud platforms have become the go-to solution for deploying and scaling AI models. They offer scalable computing power, storage, and specialized tools for AI, making it easier to manage infrastructure, optimize models, and deploy them globally. Major cloud providers such as **AWS, Google Cloud**, and **Microsoft Azure** provide comprehensive services for building and deploying AI models.

23.2.1 Key Cloud Services for AI

1. **Amazon Web Services (AWS)**: AWS offers a wide array of tools and services specifically for AI model deployment and scaling. These include **Amazon SageMaker**, which provides a fully managed environment for building, training,

and deploying machine learning models, and **AWS Lambda**, which can be used to trigger AI model inference without provisioning servers.

- o **Example**: AWS SageMaker can be used to quickly prototype a machine learning model, train it on a large dataset using distributed resources, and deploy it into production with just a few lines of code.

2. **Google Cloud Platform (GCP)**: GCP offers powerful machine learning tools like **AI Platform** for building, training, and deploying models. It also includes specialized infrastructure like **TPUs** (Tensor Processing Units) for accelerating deep learning workloads. **Google Kubernetes Engine (GKE)** helps with orchestrating containerized AI models in production.

- o **Example**: Using **AI Platform** and **Vertex AI**, Google Cloud provides a seamless way to manage machine learning workflows from development to deployment. Google also offers **BigQuery ML** for running machine learning models directly within its data warehouse environment.

3. **Microsoft Azure**: Azure's **Machine Learning Studio** allows for end-to-end management of AI models, from training to deployment. Azure also supports **Kubernetes** and **Azure Functions** for scaling machine learning models in a serverless environment. Additionally, Azure's **Cognitive Services** provides pre-built AI models for specific tasks like vision, speech, and text.

  o **Example**: Using **Azure Machine Learning**, organizations can easily deploy a model as a web service and scale it dynamically based on demand. Azure also supports **MLOps** for automating machine learning lifecycle management, including version control and model monitoring.

23.2.2 Benefits of Cloud for Scaling AI

- **Elasticity**: Cloud platforms allow for elastic scaling, meaning you can increase or decrease your compute resources depending on demand. This is crucial for applications with unpredictable or seasonal workloads.

- **Distributed Computing**: Cloud providers offer powerful distributed computing environments, such as GPU clusters and multi-node configurations, that accelerate the training and inference processes for large AI models.

- **Cost Efficiency**: Cloud computing reduces the need for upfront investment in infrastructure. Instead, organizations can pay for the resources they use, which makes scaling more cost-effective and flexible.

23.3 Case Study: Building an AI Product from Prototype to Production

Building an AI product involves several stages: **prototyping**, **scaling**, and **deployment**. In this case study, we'll walk through a simplified version of how a company might take an AI product— say, a customer sentiment analysis tool—from prototype to a fully deployed production system.

23.3.1 Stage 1: Prototyping the Model

- **Goal**: Build a sentiment analysis model to analyze customer reviews and classify them as positive, negative, or neutral.

- **Tools Used**:

  - **Python** (for developing the model)

  - **Scikit-learn** or **TensorFlow** (for building the machine learning model)

  - **Jupyter Notebook** (for exploratory analysis and experimentation)

In the prototyping stage, data is collected from various sources (e.g., customer reviews from an e-commerce platform). The data is cleaned, preprocessed, and split into training and testing sets. An initial model is developed, trained on labeled sentiment data, and evaluated using performance metrics like **accuracy** and **F1-score**.

23.3.2 Stage 2: Scaling the Model

- **Goal**: Prepare the model for deployment in a high-traffic production environment.

- **Cloud Service**: **AWS SageMaker** is used to train the model at scale, utilizing GPU instances for faster processing. The trained model is then versioned and stored in a secure model registry.

- **Deployment**: The model is deployed using **AWS Lambda**, which allows it to serve predictions without managing server infrastructure. The model is exposed via a **REST API**, enabling external applications (e.g., e-commerce platforms) to integrate it seamlessly.

23.3.3 Stage 3: Continuous Monitoring and Updates

- **Goal**: Monitor the model's performance and make updates as needed.

- **Monitoring**: The model's predictions are monitored using cloud-based logging tools, such as **AWS CloudWatch**, to track performance metrics and identify issues like **model**

drift or changes in data distribution. If performance drops, the model can be retrained with new data.

- **Updates**: As new customer reviews are collected, they are used to retrain the model periodically. This process is automated using **AWS Step Functions**, ensuring that the model stays up-to-date with minimal manual intervention.

23.3.4 Stage 4: Full-Scale Deployment

- **Goal**: Ensure the AI product can handle thousands (or millions) of simultaneous requests.

- **Infrastructure**: The model is deployed across a **load-balanced** infrastructure that scales automatically with demand, using **Elastic Load Balancing (ELB)** and **Auto Scaling** in AWS.

- **API Gateway**: The AI product is accessible through a public-facing **API Gateway**, which helps manage requests, enforce security protocols, and track usage analytics.

23.4 Conclusion

Scaling AI models for production is a multifaceted process that involves designing for performance, scalability, and continuous monitoring. Leveraging cloud services like AWS, Google Cloud, and Azure can significantly simplify and accelerate the deployment and scaling of AI models, offering on-demand compute power, storage, and specialized AI tools. By following best practices for model deployment and scaling, companies can ensure that their AI models deliver value at scale while maintaining performance, security, and reliability.

CHAPTER 24: THE FUTURE OF AI AND CONCLUSION

As artificial intelligence continues to evolve at an exponential rate, the boundaries of what is possible are being constantly pushed. In this final chapter, we will look at the emerging trends in AI research, explore career paths for those entering the AI field, and reflect on the future directions in AI applications. Understanding these trends is not only crucial for those who wish to stay ahead of the curve but also for those working to shape AI's role in society.

24.1 Emerging Trends in AI Research

The field of AI is dynamic, with several cutting-edge research areas that could significantly shape its future. Some of the most promising and exciting trends include:

24.1.1 Artificial General Intelligence (AGI)

While current AI systems excel in **narrow AI**—performing specific tasks with a high level of proficiency—**Artificial General Intelligence (AGI)** aims to build machines that can perform any intellectual task that a human being can do. AGI systems would possess a deep understanding of the world, learn from diverse experiences, and adapt to new environments much like a human.

- **Challenges**: The challenge of achieving AGI is enormous, not just from a technical standpoint, but from a **philosophical and ethical** one. Building a machine that can exhibit human-like cognitive abilities involves not only advancements in machine learning and neural networks but also the development of new theories about intelligence itself.

- **Potential Impact**: AGI could revolutionize industries by enabling machines to solve complex problems autonomously, tackle global issues like climate change, and even contribute to creative endeavors like art and music composition. However, it also raises significant risks, such as job displacement, ethical concerns about control, and the unforeseen consequences of machines with human-like capabilities.

24.1.2 Quantum Computing and AI

Quantum computing holds the potential to revolutionize AI by enabling the processing of information in ways that traditional computers cannot. Quantum computers leverage the principles of quantum mechanics, such as superposition and entanglement, to perform computations exponentially faster than classical computers.

- **Impact on AI**: For AI, quantum computing could lead to faster training of machine learning models, especially for problems that are currently intractable for classical computers. This could advance fields such as cryptography, optimization, drug discovery, and materials science. Quantum algorithms for AI have the potential to solve optimization problems, improve reinforcement learning techniques, and drastically speed up simulations.

- **Challenges**: Quantum computing is still in its infancy, and current quantum computers are not yet capable of solving practical, real-world problems at scale. However, research is advancing rapidly, and major tech companies like IBM,

Google, and Microsoft are investing heavily in quantum technologies. The intersection of quantum computing and AI will likely drive a new wave of innovation in the coming decades.

24.1.3 Explainable AI (XAI)

Explainable AI (XAI) refers to the development of AI models that are not only accurate but also interpretable by humans. As AI systems become more integrated into critical decision-making processes (e.g., healthcare, finance, legal systems), the need for transparency and accountability grows.

- **Why It Matters**: Current AI models, especially deep learning models, are often seen as "black boxes" because it can be difficult to understand how they arrive at certain decisions. XAI aims to make these models more transparent and interpretable, allowing humans to understand the reasoning behind AI's decisions and predictions.

- **Future Applications**: XAI will be crucial in fields like healthcare, where doctors need to trust and understand AI-driven diagnoses, or in finance, where regulatory bodies require transparency for automated trading systems. By improving trust in AI systems, explainable models will pave the way for broader adoption and safer applications.

24.1.4 Autonomous Systems and Robotics

The convergence of AI and robotics is rapidly transforming industries that rely on automation. From autonomous vehicles to robotic process automation (RPA), the future will see AI-driven systems playing an increasingly prominent role in both industrial and everyday tasks.

- **Autonomous Vehicles**: The development of self-driving cars continues to make headlines, with companies like Tesla, Waymo, and Uber working on AI-driven vehicles that can navigate the world without human intervention. While there are still significant technical and regulatory hurdles to overcome, the potential for reduced traffic accidents and increased efficiency is enormous.

- **Robotics in Industry**: AI-powered robots are already being used in manufacturing, agriculture, logistics, and healthcare. These systems are able to perform tasks like assembly line work, surgical assistance, and warehouse management with greater precision and efficiency than humans.

- **Challenges**: Ethical concerns surrounding automation include job displacement and the responsibility of AI systems in the event of failure (e.g., accidents caused by autonomous vehicles). Furthermore, the deployment of robots in critical industries requires robust safety standards and regulatory oversight.

24.2 Career Paths in AI Development

AI is one of the most exciting and rapidly growing fields in tech, offering a wide range of career opportunities for those with the right skills. Whether you're interested in research, development, or application, the AI industry provides a variety of paths. Here are some key roles within AI development:

24.2.1 Machine Learning Engineer

Machine learning engineers design, build, and deploy machine learning models into production systems. They are responsible for developing algorithms, optimizing models, and ensuring the models perform well at scale. A deep understanding of data structures, programming languages like Python, and machine learning frameworks like TensorFlow or PyTorch is crucial for this role.

24.2.2 Data Scientist

Data scientists analyze complex data sets to uncover trends, make predictions, and provide actionable insights. While similar to machine learning engineers, data scientists often focus more on statistical analysis, data exploration, and feature engineering, using tools like Python, R, and SQL to manipulate data and build models.

24.2.3 AI Research Scientist

AI researchers focus on advancing the field by developing new algorithms, models, and theories. This role typically requires a deep understanding of AI theory, mathematics, and computer science. Researchers often work in academia or with major tech companies like Google, Facebook, and Microsoft, contributing to the development of novel AI techniques.

24.2.4 Robotics Engineer

Robotics engineers design and build robots that integrate AI systems for autonomous operation. They often work in industries like manufacturing, logistics, healthcare, and automotive. Robotics engineers need expertise in mechanical engineering, computer science, and AI programming.

24.2.5 AI Ethics Specialist

As AI becomes more pervasive, the demand for AI ethics specialists is increasing. These professionals focus on the ethical implications of AI, ensuring that AI systems are developed and used in a way that is fair, transparent, and respects privacy. AI ethics specialists work in a range of sectors, including law, government, and academia.

- **Skills Needed**: A background in philosophy, law, or public policy, combined with technical knowledge of AI systems, is becoming more common in this role.

24.3 Final Thoughts and Future Directions in AI Applications

The future of AI holds immense potential, but it also raises complex challenges. As we continue to push the boundaries of AI's capabilities, we must ensure that these systems are developed responsibly, with a focus on transparency, fairness, and human well-being. Here are some key directions for AI's future:

1. **Collaboration with Human Intelligence**: Rather than replacing humans, AI will increasingly augment human abilities. We will see AI systems that assist professionals in various fields—doctors, lawyers, engineers, and even artists—by automating routine tasks and providing powerful insights to support decision-making.

2. **AI for Social Good**: AI has the potential to solve some of the world's most pressing issues, from climate change to poverty to healthcare access. By leveraging AI for social good, we can improve lives, drive sustainability, and promote equality.

3. **Ethical AI**: The importance of ensuring AI is ethical, transparent, and accountable will continue to grow. Efforts to mitigate bias in AI systems and develop fairer, more inclusive models will be critical for gaining public trust and ensuring that AI benefits all of humanity.

4. **AI in Creative Fields**: The fusion of AI and creativity will continue to evolve. AI is already being used to compose music, create visual art, and even write novels. As these systems become more sophisticated, they may transform how we think about authorship, creativity, and the role of technology in the arts.

5. **AI and Sustainability**: AI can play a crucial role in addressing global challenges like climate change by optimizing energy consumption, improving resource management, and advancing clean technologies. The synergy between AI and environmental sustainability will be a defining theme of the next decade.

The future of AI is both exciting and uncertain. As AI systems become increasingly sophisticated, they will have a transformative impact on industries, economies, and societies. However, as with any powerful technology, the risks and ethical considerations must be managed responsibly. By fostering interdisciplinary collaboration, prioritizing ethical development, and embracing AI's potential for good, we can shape a future where AI contributes positively to humanity's collective well-being.

The journey toward a more intelligent world has only just begun, and the possibilities for AI are as vast as our imagination. The only certainty is that AI will continue to challenge our understanding of intelligence, autonomy, and what it means to be human.

www.ingramcontent.com/pod-product-compliance
Lightning Source LLC
LaVergne TN
LVHW022335060326
832902LV00022B/4055